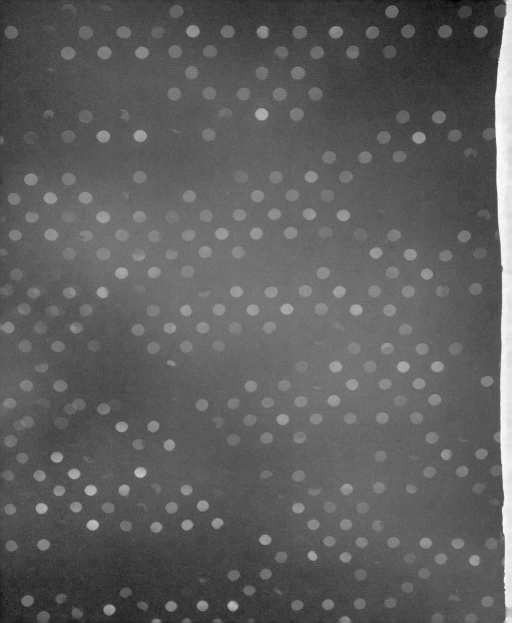

SASSY, CLASSY, AND STILL *Sparkling*

CELEBRATING LIFE AFTER 50

All Scripture references are taken from the *New King James Version* ©
1979, 1980, 1982, 1992, by Thomas Nelson, Inc.

Published in Nashville, Tennessee, by Thomas Nelson, Inc.
Thomas Nelson is a registered trademark of Thomas Nelson, Inc.

Managing Editor: Lisa Stilwell
Project Editor: Jessica Inman
Designed by Koechel Peterson & Associates, Inc., Minneapolis, MN

ISBN-10: 1-4041-0520-4
ISBN-13: 978-1-4041-0520-1

Printed and bound in China

www.thomasnelson.com

SASSY, CLASSY, AND STILL *Sparkling*

CELEBRATING LIFE AFTER 50

THOMAS NELSON
Since 1798

by Ruby Red Hat

NASHVILLE   DALLAS   MEXICO CITY   RIO DE JANEIRO   BEIJING

Table of Contents

STILL SPARKLING 51

HEARTS OF GOLD 93

LAUGH LINES 107

FRIENDSHIP GETS BETTER AFTER FIFTY 139

INTRODUCTION

*O*nce upon a time, women approaching fifty and beyond were invisible—marginalized by the same society that invented tombstone-shaped cakes, black balloons, and "Over the Hill" banners. We've all had younger relatives point out that forty is halfway to eighty and fifty is halfway to one hundred. Back then, when you started approaching "a certain age," people seemed to expect you to quietly accept your fate, fading away to the margins.

But as The Red Hat Society celebrates its tenth birthday, we can proudly proclaim that women at midlife and beyond are no longer marginalized—but are now sought after! Simply by getting together to laugh, have a good time, and embrace ourselves as the dazzling divas we truly are, we have turned the notions of what it means to be a woman fifty, seventy, or ninety years old on its head. In fact, our red hats and purple boas have sent a message to all sectors of society, in countries around the globe, that we are a force for the good with which to reckon. We have evolved, in fact, into the pivotal social movement redefining traditional notions of aging for women around the world.

It all started ten years ago when founder Sue Ellen Cooper gave her friend Linda Murphy a red hat along with a framed copy of the poem "Warning" by Jenny Joseph, which begins, "When I am an old woman I shall wear purple / With a red hat which doesn't go, and doesn't suit me." It wasn't long before the two friends decided to join others for tea, all wearing red hats with purple outfits. From there the group grew to a healthy size, a number of women "of a certain age" who wanted to get together regularly and embrace middle age and beyond with humor, spunk, and sparkle. And their numbers only grew. That small group at a tea table is now a global sisterhood—and it's not uncommon to see entire hotels filled with women in red hats.

In our new world, the fiftieth birthday party is no longer a time to mope. In fact, as one of our pre-fifty members excitedly anticipates approaching "the birthday" (members under fifty wear pink hats until they "come of age"), she can expect a wild and festive "*red*uation," a rite of passage and a celebration of her entrance into what could be the wildest, craziest, most fun phase of her life yet, full of red feather boas and decadent desserts.

We're about wearing wild high heels and lots of jewelry, hopping in the car for another great adventure, and long, leisurely teas. So what's not to love about being fifty?

We hope these stories will make you laugh, make you happy, and help you think of ways to celebrate yourself as the sassy, classy woman you are. May you find your own "*hat*titude" and a new lease on life.

Ruby RedHat

LIVING LIFE WITH SASS

What is sass, you ask? Sass is that almost indefinable quality that's a little like confidence and a lot like spunk. Sass is a look-at-me outfit, a little backtalk when necessary, and boldly going after not only what you want but what the world needs more of. Just listen to these sassy ladies share their stories of living life with attitude. You'll be in touch with your inner diva in no time.

What is sass?

Two HALVES MAKE MORE THAN a WHOLE

What soap is to the body,
laughter is to the soul.

YIDDISH PROVERB

Growing up, I hated that my birthday fell in December. With Christmas just days apart from my birthday, I only received presents once a year. Even as an adult, with the hustle and bustle of the holiday season, I found it almost impossible to make time for a birthday celebration. For years I tried to nudge my kids toward celebrating my half birthday in June, but my efforts were to no avail.

Finally, at a bunco gathering, I declared to everyone present that I would be celebrating my half birthday this year—the last birthday before age sixty-five should be celebrated fully, I reasoned. And so, as June approached, I sent an e-mail to all of my fellow bunco babes decreeing that June's bunco night would instead be a birthday party celebrating another member's full birthday and my half birthday.

"Let me handle the details," a friend said. "You don't need to be worrying about all the food and what to bring since you're getting ready to go on a trip—and it is your birthday party, after all!"

"If you insist," I told her.

I knew that this group, such imaginative, creative, and quick-witted ladies, would put great effort into planning a positively brilliant half birthday party. Just thinking about what they might be plotting gave me the giggles.

When I arrived on the big night, I saw that my expectations would be more than met. All the ladies were dressed according to the "half" theme, each one with her own interpretation. One came half dressed for bed, with a regular shoe on one foot and a bedroom slipper on the other. One lady—who never showed a naughty side as far as I could tell—dressed as half good, half naughty. Her left sleeve was rolled up to reveal drawn-on tattoos, and on her right hand she wore her usual jewelry.

Even the food fit the theme. I saw half a watermelon, and someone served half a gallon of half sweet tea. There was half a bottle of wine, semicircle-shaped cookies, and chicken salad served in half slices of pita bread. There were deviled eggs (no halving necessary) and half sandwiches. The birthday cake—a half sheet—read "Happy

> Just thinking about what they might be plotting gave me the giggles. And when I arrived on the big night, I saw that my expectations would be more than met.

Birthday" to the birthday girl on one side; the other side read "Hap Birt Ju," which is half of each word of "Happy Birthday Judy." My creative hostesses served the food on half plates, and name cards were cut in half so that we went around calling each other by the first syllable or so of our names.

When the time came to open presents, I found that my birthday cards were all cut in half. I received a decorative coffee cup with a note that read "half a cup." It was literally half a cup—it had been sliced down the center. I opened a half dollar from the year I was born, one red earring paired with one purple earring, and a mismatched pair of socks (I bet there's another pair just like it somewhere).

Their ideas seemed to go on and on. This celebration far outpaced any other I had ever attended; I loved celebrating my birthday without the pressure of trying to make sure everyone in my family was having a good Christmas. So from that warm June evening forward, I have celebrated my half birthday with my friends and my full birthday with my family.

Two birthday parties—what a great way to enjoy each year.

Judy Bloss
Vintage Gals, Alachua, Florida,
and Bunco Babes of
Gainesville, Florida

Centuries of Sass

Just in case you had any doubt about what sassy women are capable of, history gives us countless examples of women whose sass led them into legendary exploits:

 The life of Cleopatra has spawned elaborate legends and more than a few films. We can't be historically sure that she really did dissolve a pearl in vinegar and drink it in order to win a bet over Antony, but we do know that she wielded considerable power and that her beauty was legendary. So we can only assume that she was politically savvy and knew when to get a little cheeky.

Historians may debate the net gains and losses of Elizabeth I's rule, but there's no question that she fended off threats to her reign and to her subjects with a measure of guts and gumption. The Virgin Queen has fascinated us for centuries, becoming an icon for fiery redheads everywhere.

Harriet Tubman defied the status quo by helping more than 300 slaves escape to freedom.
She also reportedly planned and executed a raid
that freed over 750 slaves at once. Her special
combination of defiance and kindness proved
that a woman with a mission can change the
course of history.

Embracing a spirit of sass just might put a little lift in our spirits
and make the day ahead seem even brighter with possibilities.
Who knows what might happen when we put a little attitude in
our step?

We might
even *change*
the world.

The PURPLE TRUCK

You don't know what you can get away with until you try.

COLIN POWELL

*A*s the day of our town's Christmas parade drew closer, one of our members, Claudia, grew determined that our Red Hat Society chapter would not only participate but leave an impression no one in town would ever forget. She got on the phone and found that many of our thirty-five members wouldn't be home over the Thanksgiving weekend and thus were unavailable. Not to be discouraged, Claudia sent an e-mail to those of us who could make it, asking us to meet her at a nearby car wash at 9:00 a.m. the day before the parade.

Only five of us showed up to prepare her husband's truck for the parade. And all five of our mouths dropped open when Claudia pulled out large jars of purple poster paint. We would paint Mat's truck purple for the parade, including the tires, Claudia insisted. A little shocked, we snickered as we got to work with sponge brushes.

And soon, unbeknownst to Mat, he was the owner of one very purple automobile.

We hid the truck overnight and woke up early to decorate it with a large red hat that Claudia had made. And then we took our place in the parade lineup. I, the queen mum, rode on top of the cab, and the other Rouge-ettes rode in the truck bed while Claudia drove.

> He looked thoughtful and responded, "I smell ... **purple.**"

We needed no music to accompany our float: we played "Jingle Bells" with plenty of gusto on our kazoos, which I think the kids watching the parade enjoyed. Men standing along the parade route broke into laughter when they saw the truck. One yelled out, "Where'd you get the purple truck?" and we replied, "It's her husband's! He doesn't know we painted it." He fell to the ground laughing—or crying, we weren't sure which. Maybe he was picturing his own wife painting his truck purple.

Claudia's goal of making a splash had definitely been met. When the parade was over, the six of us went directly to the car wash, with just a little trepidation, to see if the paint would wash off. We breathed a sigh of relief when we saw the purple paint filling the drains. We couldn't quite get the pink shoe polish off the tires, though, and we worried about what would happen to Claudia if Mat discovered what we did to his precious truck.

The next morning, Mat and Claudia got into the truck to make a trip to the store. Mat began sniffing exaggeratedly as if trying to find the source of a smell. "What on earth are you sniffing for?" Claudia asked.

He looked thoughtful and responded, "I smell . . . purple."

Lesson learned: you can't fool a man you've lived with for nearly fifty years. He knows you better than you think he does. We also learned later that the water at the car wash is recycled. When Claudia heard this, she said to our group, "Just picture a white Ferrari coming out of the car wash with purple streaks."

That's us: desecrating vehicles of all makes and models. Wherever we go, we like to leave a memorable mark, preferably a purple one.

Barbara Stelloh
Les Rouge-ettes,
Emerald Isle,
North Carolina

The POWER of ATTITUDE

*Just around the corner in every woman's **mind** is a lovely dress, a wonderful suit, or entire costume which will make an **enchanting** new creature of her.*

WILHELA CUSHMAN

It was Red Hat Society Day in our town, and the morning had dawned beautiful and sunny and just a little crisp. Three of us from my newly formed chapter were enjoying a day of shopping, laughing, and dressing up in our town's historic district with other Red Hat chapters. For the occasion, lots of merchants had hung Red Hat Society flags, and we saw welcoming signs galore.

We made the rounds looking in windows and exulting over bargains. Suddenly I spied a beautifully dressed window and stopped in my tracks. High on one shelf was the most beautiful red hat I had ever seen. It had a wide brim and long, arching feathers, and reminded me of the Gibson Girls my grandmother had told me about long ago. I absolutely had to have it, so I went inside and purchased it along with a sassy boa, and for the rest of the morning, I strutted my stuff.

Lunchtime quickly rolled around, and it was time to catch a shuttle to a nearby restaurant, where we'd gather with the other Red Hatters. In all the excitement, when I boarded the shuttle bus, I unknowingly left my purse on an iron bench, and I didn't even realize it until we got to the restaurant and I needed my glasses to check the afternoon itinerary.

We notified the police, but somehow I just couldn't get upset. I was having the time of my life with my new hat and boa. The German band was playing the chicken dance song, and my chapter queen, Julie, was dancing on the table. Who could worry about a missing purse at a time like this?

After lunch, I bustled over to one of the merchants, who had arranged to have a telephone available for me to call my credit card companies and all of that. But as I started dialing, I heard other Red Hatters calling my name. A handsome young police-man appeared in their midst, smiling from ear to ear, sporting a light blush, and swinging my purse in his right hand. I ran to him and thanked him, and as I looked through my bag, I discovered that everything was in place—not a thing was missing. The shop-ping could go on.

> The band was playing the chicken dance song, and my chapter queen, Julie, was dancing on the table. Who could worry about a missing purse at a time like this?

I hugged him and thanked him several more times, and he smiled and said softly, "You have a good afternoon." And I knew that the rest of the day would be even better than the morning.

It's funny how some extravagant attire can make you impervious to the stresses of life. That hat and boa—along with the laughter of friends and the dutiful work of a fine young police officer—made my day wholly, completely wonderful. Even a lost purse couldn't ruffle my feathers.

Denise Lucas
The Sisters of the Red and Pink Hats, Covington, Kentucky

It Never Rains on My Parade

Things turn out **best**
for the people who make the best
of the way things turn out.

ART LINKLETTER

My women's group had made plans to march in the local Christmas parade in December of 2005, and we all looked forward to wowing the crowd in our festive outfits. But rain fell heavily on the morning of the parade, so the other ladies decided to withdraw.

Unfortunately, I (the group's official "Honorary Ornery") didn't get the message. So I showed up at the parade and became confused when I didn't see any of my friends there. I asked around and found out that they had cancelled.

I stuck my lips out in a pout. I figured I should probably just go home, but I was all dressed up and not ready to give up just yet. And then I spied an opportunity. A herd of motorcycles pulled up beside me to assume their position in the parade lineup, representing the Apostles Motorcycle Ministry, which I hadn't heard of until just then.

I approached one of the drivers and asked sweetly if I could ride on his cycle. He looked surprised, but agreed with a smile. I hopped on the back of his Harley, and then off we were. As I blew bubbles along the parade route, we turned a few heads, I must say, and my driver didn't seem to mind.

None of my friends or family members were surprised when I related this little tale. They know me well: if there's fun to be had, I'm going to find it, and no rain is going to stop me.

Judie Carbaugh
The Hat'Attudes,
Safety Harbor,
Florida

The ART OF MISBEHAVING

If you obey all the rules,

you miss all the fun.

KATHERINE HEPBURN

While visiting a friend in Texas, I saw a group of colorful, fun-having ladies who filled nearly half a restaurant, and someone explained to me why they got together the way they did. This was my first introduction to Red Hatting, and these gorgeous ladies enthralled me. Five weeks later, after I'd returned to England, I found myself sitting at an inaugural get-together with other women wearing purple dresses with red hats that didn't go.

We dreamed big at this first meeting. Our chapter began with the goal to practice behaving badly now that we were over fifty, and we even appointed a monitor to see that all good behavior was discouraged. We started the meeting with some silly get-to-know-each-other games, and then we started coming up with ideas of things to do and places to go to continue all types of disgraceful behavior. We planned to go to the races and the theater; enjoy

> We wanted to practice behaving badly now that we were over fifty; we even appointed a monitor to see that all good behavior was discouraged.

dinners out as often as we wanted; attend high tea at posh hotels; share books; learn new skills; go horseback riding and hot air ballooning and maybe even dry slope skiing.

Each member was given a little vial of bubbles to blow instead of applauding, a kazoo on which to play "Happy Birthday" (we quickly discovered that we needed a little more practice), purple bangles, a red sash, a red notebook with a red pencil and pencil case for dreaming up mischief, and a few purple-wrapped sweets.

We instituted a red box near the entrance so that all unhappy thoughts could be left at the door, and determined that at further meetings, a "happy bunny" would be available to hug any gloomy Gus until she was a happy bunny again.

I doubt, though, that we'll need the happy bunny all too often. With wild friends like these bent on having all kinds of fun and misbehaving as often as possible, I'm sure we'll be laughing way too much to be grumpy.

Wendy Pott
The Oakley Red Hat
Lax Bloomers,
Hampshire, England

Some PEOPLE JUST DON'T UNDERSTAND

Be *yourself.* *No one can*
ever tell you you're doing it wrong.

AUTHOR UNKNOWN

We Red Hatters might as well face it: we're bright red targets. Go out in public in a red hat and a feather boa and you're bound to attract a certain amount of attention and draw a certain number of comments—good, bad, and sometimes a little obtuse.

I've done retail sales, so I'm accustomed to unsolicited comments. In my younger life, I demonstrated food processors at Macy's, pulverizing more fresh veggies than I care to remember. Chopping cabbage, shredding carrots, and slicing cucumbers elicited a stream of annoyingly stale jokes from shoppers who operated under the misguided notion that they were amazingly clever. I have no idea how often I heard things like, "It chops. It slices. It dices. We didn't need to go to the restaurant for lunch, honey. We could have eaten here." Har, har.

Their quips were neither unique nor humorous, but that didn't stop these wannabe comics from guffawing at their own pathetic wit while noshing on chopped, sliced, and diced veggies (usually double dipping too, but we won't go there).

So I shouldn't be surprised at the comments people make during a Red Hat gathering. Here are a few of my favorites:

"Are you one of those Red Hat ladies?" This, of course, is the most common. It is also the most silly, if you think about it. No one who's not a Red Hatter dresses the way we do. Certainly our outfits vary from lady to lady, but the overall uniform shouts, "Red Hat!" It's like asking a Girl Scout if she's a Girl Scout or a marine if he's a marine. But anytime I'm asked, I say yes, I'm a Red Hat lady.

"Oooh. Red Hat ladies. Can we take your picture?" Whoever heard of taking a picture of complete strangers? Are we a novelty act? And what do these people do with the photos they take of us? When company comes over, do they drag out our pictures along with their Disneyland slides and Halloween photos of their grandkids?

I'm really complaining unnecessarily: the truth is that I've yet to meet a Red Hatter who isn't eager to mug for the camera at any time. After all, we're at our cutest in full regalia, so why not ham it up for our adoring public?

"Are you ladies together?" I love this one. It usually is asked by a member of the wait staff when we're waiting for a table at a restaurant. The last time it happened, four of us were standing in a foyer with about eight other people. The others were dressed like plain folk; we Red Hatters, on the other hand, were adorned in our finest Red Hat attire. Chatting, giggling, and indiscreetly scanning the walls

> Go out in public in a bright red hat and a feather boa and you're bound to attract a certain amount of attention and draw a certain number of comments—good, bad, and sometimes a little obtuse.

for a "restroom" sign, we were the only ones dressed in look-alike purple dresses and red hats, rather like oversized quadruplets whose mother dressed them in matching clothes. It was quite safe to assume that, yes, all of us ladies were together.

"What's your agenda?" I'm not making this up. A yuppie-looking thirty-something posed this question as a group of us munched yeast rolls at a restaurant. I'm not sure he believed me when I explained that our only agenda was food, fun, and fellowship. Too bad there aren't any Red Hat men. This fellow needed to lighten up and learn to have fun. He was way too serious and way too suspicious.

Lest you think I'm cynical, I must share that being a Red Hatter draws wonderful comments too. I love it when a toddler points at me and coos, "Pretty." And I get all mushy inside when a little girl looks at me with eyes as big as saucers. I'm sure she doesn't see me as an adult but as a grown-up little girl who enjoys playing dress-up as much as she does (which I do).

The best comments are unspoken. They are the smiles on people's faces when Red Hatters enter a room. They are the giggles and pointing fingers of little boys and girls. They are the looks of appreciation on gentlemen's faces, men who see women as God's most beautiful creations, especially when we are dressed in regal finery.

There are people who don't get it, and there are people who do get it: sassy, classy ladies who embrace life and look for the fun in everything are a splash of color in a sometimes monotone world.

"Are you a Red Hat lady?" You betcha—I'm on a mission to live life big, and I'm declaring it with a bright red hat and a purple boa. Any comments?

Donna Rogers
Hornet Hatters,
Kansas City,
Missouri

CLASSY DAMES

One of the great things about getting older is realizing how the years have molded us into refined, elegant women. In the pages to come, you'll meet smart, beautiful, accomplished gals who serve their communities, defy all limitations, and dress like a million bucks. There's nothing quite as classy as a dame who's been around for a few years.

Defy all limitations

The CLOSET

The *great* *thing about*
getting older is that you don't lose
all the other ages you've been.

MADELEINE L'ENGLE

When I was a little girl, my mother was a model. Not a runway model, but a print ad and TV commercial model. Back then, if you booked a print or commercial job, you were told what kind of look the client had in mind and were expected to bring a selection of your own clothes to each shoot. Obviously, this necessitated quite a wardrobe on the part of the models, and many times they had to go out and purchase the clothing required for a particular job.

So you can imagine the varied and beautiful contents of my mother's closet and jewelry drawers. As a little girl I would stand in her closet in awe—evening gowns, furs, hats, shoes, all assorted things in all colors and fabrics. There was glittery stuff, velvety stuff, hats with feathers, shoes that glittered. One huge drawer held jewelry of every color and every style, from casual to elegant. There were long gloves, short gloves, hair pieces, and false eyelashes. I imagined that hers had to be the most amazing collection in the world.

None of my friends' mothers had closets like this, of course. My friends would come over and marvel at the clothes with me. We all peeked inside the closet door as if it led to a cave full of treasures, and if we could get away with it, you better believe we tried everything on.

> My closet held only sensible clothing for work, a couple of not-so-intriguing Sunday dresses, and sensible shoes, nothing any little girl would be too interested in—nothing that I was too interested in.

All of this made me think that my mother was important. Maybe I wouldn't have said so exactly, but I thought that my mother was a woman of substance and a little bit of intrigue. If you were interesting, I reasoned, if you were important, if you had a fabulous job, then you had a closet like hers. I believed it to my core.

I grew up, got married, had a child, had a job, and did all the things that women do. My closet held only sensible clothing for work, a couple of not-so-intriguing Sunday dresses, and sensible shoes, nothing any little girl would be too interested in—nothing that I was too interested in. My child grew up and moved away and I started working at home, and my world shrunk to an even smaller place than before.

Looking for friends, or at least a lunch out every now and then, I started a Red Hat Society chapter with a girlfriend. The Red Rubies soon evolved into a group of twenty-two best friends who are so busy we sometimes don't have time to breathe. And we love it.

After four years as a Red Hatter, I recently stopped in my tracks in the middle of my closet. I had come in to get something, found it, and turned out the light. And then I turned it on again and took a look around. In that moment I realized something wonderful: I had an interesting closet. With a growing sense of satisfaction, I admired my feather boas, my sequined jackets, my evening gowns, my completely non-sensible shoes bought solely on the basis of their color and the generous "bling" on the straps. And my hats, those glorious red hats. I have hat boxes, but there are always a few loose hats on the shelves, and there they were, each one more beautiful than the other, each with a memory of where it had been worn.

I went over to my jewelry drawer to take a look, and I saw that it had its own fabulousness as well. My group attends a lot of fun events, and if there is a theme for the day, we buy all the jewelry we can find that fits the theme. As a result, I have jewelry suited

> I admired my feather boas, my sequined jackets, my evening gowns, my completely non-sensible shoes, bought solely on the basis of their color and the generous "bling" on the straps.

for all kinds of themes, some of it cheap and gaudy, some of it expensive and extravagant, and all of it dearly loved.

The thrill I felt came not just from realizing that I had an interesting closet—and thus, that I must be a woman of substance—but also from rediscovering the little girl I had been. The same things that made her sigh and filled her with awe still did so for the grown-up me. She had somehow reemerged during the last four years.

It was she who bought those feather boas, the tiaras, all those hats.

She is the one who signed up to float down the Chattahoochee River on a tube and lose all her adult pride, who giggled for three hours straight with her vice queen, the Lady of Enthusiasm (Thusey to her friends), because we were stuck on rocks and had to wait for assistance.

She is the one who agreed to play paintball, something the grown-up me would never have even considered.

As I stood in my closet, I knew that I would never again be that woman who got so bogged down in adulthood and responsibilities that she forgot how to laugh. I knew that I would spend the rest of my life as a vibrant, funny, interesting, engaging woman who knew who she was and what she wanted. And I knew, without a doubt, that I would always, as long as I lived, have an interesting closet.

Ruth Hodge
The Red Rubies,
Dacula, Georgia

A TOP COP

Consider the postage stamp:
its usefulness consists
in the ability to stick
to one thing till it gets there.

With almost thirty years in law enforcement under her belt, one might think the first and only female police chief in the history of Chester County, Pennsylvania, would be slowing down. But Deidre Sherman still gets a thrill out of police work. "I tell everyone that I've been here three days longer than dirt," she says. "But I still love my job, and you still get that same feeling of satisfaction when you solve a crime or make an arrest."

She could have gone several ways when it came to career choices. She holds degrees in French and sociology, but during her studies she happened to take a criminal defense class, and that's when she was "bitten by the law enforcement bug." She started pursuing a career in law right away.

Step one was the police academy. After graduating, she moved on to step two and began pounding the pavement for jobs as an officer. But even after six years of applying, she had yet to land a job. Still, she wasn't ready to give up.

When she interviewed with the Spring City Police Department, she landed first among the other applicants in written and oral exams, but she experienced a setback when she lost the position to another candidate because he had previous patrolling experience. And then there was a breakthrough: the department head left, leaving a spot open for Deidre, and she began her first full-time patrolling job.

Twenty years later, she was named police chief.

That same month, she received devastating news: a diagnosis of breast cancer. But she was determined to go forward as police chief. She manned her post four days a week, receiving treatment on her off days. "I had worked so long to become a police chief, and it was so important to me," she said. "I was bound and determined for so long that I wasn't going to let anything keep me from achieving that goal." Despite the exhaustion she suffered due to the cancer treatments, she kept going. And her perseverance paid

> I was bound and determined for so long that I wasn't going to let anything keep me from achieving that goal.

off—she's cancer free today, thanks to her strong support system, she says.

Deidre's life post-cancer is full. She loves her family—her husband and stepson—and she loves her work. "It's hard to pin down just one thing I love about law enforcement," she says. "Every day is different." She's a classic example of a high-class lady who pursues her dreams—in any stage of life, in any circumstances—with tenacity and guts. And she has a rich life to show for her efforts.

Deidre Sherman
R.H. Factor, Spring City, Pennsylvania

The ABCs of Red Hatting

AFFIRMING: Red Hatters affirm each other. We recognize that we have all traveled many diverse roads but, for some reason or other, have been brought together in the same place and time. And we celebrate and encourage each other—past, present, and future. We appreciate our maturity and believe that together we can let the coming generations know that life does not stop at forty.

BELIEVING: Red Hatters believe in the worth of others—old, young, male, female—and ourselves. Like Peter Pan and Tinkerbell, we must believe in order to maintain our youthful existence. (Say it with me: "I believe in fairies. I believe in fairies.")

CARING: When life knocks one Red Hatter down, the others flock to her for support. Red Hatters are there to celebrate the joys of life and to offer comfort in its difficulties.

DARING: If you want to be a Red Hatter, an ornery, daredevil streak is a requirement. Dressing up in purple outfits and red hats and parading around in public is not for the meek.

EXPERIENCED: We have a wealth of experiences as mothers, spouses, business-people, daughters, teachers, doctors, nurses, homemakers, lawyers, pilots, laborers, ministers, secretaries, and of course friends. And the advantage of our collective years of experience is that no matter what happens, at least one of us has done it before and knows what it's like.

FUN: If you want to have fun, join a Red Hat group. If you are a stick in the mud, don't bother attending a meeting; you'll be miserable the whole time.

We are joyful that the sun rose, the car started, the dog pottied outside, and the trash man came. The older we become, the more we find to be joyful about.

GIVING: Red Hatters give. We give love, we give support, we give joy, we give energy—where else but a Red Hat get-together can you find such giving?

HAT: And then of course there is the hat, which, as we know, can be anything worn on the head—visors, ball caps, cowboy hats, tiaras, any type of chapeau that declares your affiliation with the Red Hatters.

IMPERFECT: Desperate housewives need not apply. Red Hatters understand dust, piles of laundry, unshaved legs, cookie crumbs from grandchildren's visits, empty ice cream pints, no makeup, McDonald's sacks on the floor of the car, an occasional curse word . . .

JOYFUL: Red Hatters celebrate. We are joyous because today we woke up and are alive; we are joyful that the sun rose, the car started, the dog pottied outside, and the trash man came. The older we become, the more we find to be joyful about.

*K*INDRED: There is a connection, a kindred spirit, among Red Hatters. Maybe it's because we are truly survivors—forget reality TV; we have reality lives.

*L*OVING: Red Hatters share a heart connection, a love that can't be explained. We are experts at loving, having given love all our lives—to our families, friends, neighbors, homes, and sometimes even our jobs. When Red Hatters get together, you can feel the love.

*M*ATURE: Hallelujah! My mother always said I need to be more mature, and now I think I've made it: I am mature! Of course, I don't think that was the kind of maturity she was speaking of. Last summer, I went to the doctor with abdominal pain. He apologized for doing so many tests, but even though he suspected appendicitis, he wanted to test for other things as well because—long pause—"mature women usually don't have appendicitis."

*N*AUGHTY: Most of us enjoy being a wee bit naughty sometimes, and as Red Hatters we have an excuse: we're "mature." We are past the age of being told to behave, but not past the age of caring about our sexuality. What a fun place to be! We're not talking about anything major, just an occasional dirty joke or a little flirting with the waiter. As Helen Reddy said, "I am woman. Hear me roar."

*O*PEN: No secrets here, girls. It may seem a little like gossip, but most of the time it's just plain caring. We want to hear about what each other is experiencing so we can be there for them.

*P*LAYFUL: Folks, we have spent our lives making sure our families had some fun, our children had their play dates, our spouses got their down time, and our work was done, whether inside or outside the home. And now it's our turn to play. Play cards, go to plays, play dress-up. You have to be playful to get the full benefit of being a Red Hatter.

QUIRKY: Along those same lines, we get to be a little quirkier now (not that we weren't quirky in the past). People excuse our quirks because—again—we are "mature" women. 🌹

RUGGED: On a more serious note, we also have to be rugged. We have weathered many storms throughout our mature lives, and there are many more to come. We have lost children, coworkers, friends, parents, spouses. We have lost homes, jobs, and sometimes our health. We have survived, we're still strong, and when we can't be, we have our Red Hat sisters to support us. 🌹

SHARING: We share. We share stories, jokes, e-mails, clothes, jewelry, hats, pictures of grandkids, vacations, you name it. 🌹

TOLERANT: We are so diverse that if we weren't tolerant, we wouldn't exist. We are tolerant because we know that diversity among individuals only enhances the whole group. 🌹

Folks, we have spent our lives making sure our families had some fun, our children had their play dates, our spouses got their down time, and our work was done. And now it's our turn to play.

UNDERSTANDING: There is a bond among Red Hatters that transcends speech. A look, a touch, a brief note or e-mail can communicate volumes. 🌹

VITAL: To thrive at our age, a person has to have life in her veins. To be a Red Hatter, you don't have to be able to run around the block or anything; you just have to have an appreciation for the goodness in life. Despite all the annoying problems that come with "maturity," it sure beats the alternative. 🌹

WRINKLED: Enough said. No one is allowed to be a Red Hatter unless they have one wrinkle. And your shirt doesn't count. 🌹

X-RAYED: Anyone in the Red Hat Society has surely had at least one X–ray in her life. We've experienced the cold slab, the immodest garments, the scary compressing plates, and the sci-fi noises that accompany an X–ray.

YOUTHFUL: Wrinkled, yet young and youthful at heart is all that is needed here. No reason to give up on youth just because your body insists you do so.

ZANY: You have to be just a little bit zany if you're going to do the crazy things you wish you had done when you were younger, when you could have done them better, looked better, and just plain felt better. At least now you're finally getting around to doing those zany things.

So there it is in a nutshell, the essence of what it means to be a Red Hatter. Of course there are no rules to our society per se, but I think we'd all agree that we are, in our wonderful, zany, diverse ways, amazingly similar. We're drawn together across the miles by our love for each other and our determination to act as young as we feel. The way we see it, we've earned the right to have a good time.

So whatever color your hat is, don't be afraid to let your hair down every now and then.

Raise a *glass* to yourself and all the fun-loving ladies you know.

Libby Sanders
The Jewels of Denial,
Salem, Missouri

Funny that a pair of
really nice shoes make us
feel good in our heads—at the extreme
opposite end of our bodies.

LEVENDE WATERS

There are certain things a sassy, classy woman never leaves home without:

 Lipstick. For flirting, leaving a lasting impression, and general attention-getting.

 Hairstylist's phone number. For emergencies.

 Glamorous companions. To step in as comedians, dispensers of wisdom, dance partners, and dessert-sharers.

 Compact. For makeup touchups—and tweezing the occasional rogue hair.

Rumpled receipts dating back to 1996. Because a classy lady is mindful of the state of her bank account, if not the state of her purse.

 Handbag. A fabulous one, if possible. For storing other necessities of class.

Many elements of class can't fit in a purse, of course. A certain grace and fearlessness accompany every classy lady, along with resourcefulness and a willingness to make others feel like classy guys and dolls in their own right. When you've met a classy dame, you'll know it, if not by her lipstick, then by her smile.

SHARING
the WEALTH

*Act as if what you do makes
a* **difference.** *It does.*

WILLIAM JAMES

It all started with a group of volunteers at the Seasons of Life Hospice in Parma, Ohio. As we worked alongside each other, I watched and was inspired as these volunteers gave of themselves in countless ways. They listened to the life stories of the dying— mostly stories about loving and being loved. They listened to the fears of family members as they faced a future without their mother or father or husband or wife. They simply held a hand or gave a drink of water. They ran errands and picked up prescriptions. They stayed the afternoon or evening so that family members could go to the grocery store or go to graduations or simply go out to dinner. They prayed with and for those who were dying. They tried to make each day a good day.

As we worked together, our friendship grew, and we decided to form our very own chapter of the Red Hat Society. And soon we were meeting once a month to do something new and different. One month was a pajama party; we spent the night in a log cabin eating tasty treats and playing dominoes, walking in the woods and swatting mosquitoes, and then eating some more. Another month, we went to see a live show called *Menopause the Musical*, where we laughed until we cried. We had lunch in Amish country and did a little shopping. We've had numerous potlucks. (You'll notice that food is a recurring motif in our get-togethers.) We had high tea at a fancy hotel for Christmas, all of us elegantly attired in beautiful dresses and long gloves. We love to spoil ourselves with fun and frivolity.

But we want to share our joy with others, and that's why at each of our events, we pass around a hat. From January to June, we collect money and purchase items for Malachi House, a nonprofit home for the terminally ill. Malachi House residents have less than six months to live, no caregivers, no insurance, and no money. At Malachi, they are provided with a private room, home-cooked meals, and the love and support of a trained staff with help from volunteers. All services are provided solely by donations.

One of the hospice volunteers, Audrey, also volunteers at Malachi House. She purchases items from the money we collect, including toiletries, paper towels, and canned goods, and we deliver all the items at their Christmas in July party.

We want to **share** our joy with others, and that's why at each of our events, we pass around a hat.

From July to December, the money we collect goes to the Berea Children's Home. This group of people runs more programs than I can count—they provide resources for mental and behavioral health, summer camps, child care, and a variety of educational programs and alternative schooling, and they also help with adoption and foster care. The children they help need clothing and toys, and their families can use just about everything imaginable.

One of our members, Palma, is the greatest shopper ever, so we enlist her to put our money to good use for the children's home. She once managed to buy almost a thousand dollars' worth of clothing for about $150. She continues to shop, and we continue to donate money and needed items to the Berea Children's Home, delivering our gifts at Christmastime. It's something our group looks forward to every year.

This group of ladies initially met through bringing peace and comfort to the last days of others, and we came together out of our desire to make our own lives rich and full—which includes being silly. But for us, it also includes spreading our joy and making life a little easier for others. We've found that life gets even better when we share the wealth of laughter and fun.

Mary Kennard
Red Hot Hatties,
Parma, Ohio

STILL SPARKLING

Just because we've had that significant birthday doesn't mean we're ready for a rocking chair. We have all kinds of surprises up our sleeves; it's never too late to do something new and exciting, adopt a fashionable new hairstyle, or take that risk we never had the courage to take before. As you read these ladies' sparkling stories, you just might think of new goals and dreams or new ways to celebrate your own special sparkle.

New and exciting

DREAM BIG

You are never too old to set another goal or to dream a new dream.

C. S. LEWIS

When I was in high school in the sixties, I went to see the school guidance counselor for . . . well, guidance, I guess. His job was to help us translate our areas of interest into meaningful, profitable careers. I think that was part of his job description, anyway.

He asked me the perfunctory question confronting many sixteen-year-olds: "What do you want to do when you grow up?" Actually, I knew exactly what I wanted to do. Amelia Earhart was one of my earliest heroines and role models. I had read her biography several times, each time growing more inspired by her strength, courage, and audacity. (Although I don't think my vocabulary included the word *audacity* at the time.)

I wanted to be just like her. Even her disappearance seemed to have romantic possibilities and a distinct cachet. I never pictured her in a watery grave; I imagined that she decided to drop out of the public eye and live out her life on a remote Pacific island, worshipped as a goddess.

And so, when the guidance counselor asked me what I wanted to do for the rest of my life, I told him I wanted to be an airline pilot. He looked at me and said very knowingly (and patronizingly, I felt), "You mean you want to be a stewardess." (That's what we called flight attendants back then.)

Of course, the Elaine of today would have told the man exactly what she thought of his suggestion, but at the time I was just sixteen and bowed to what I thought was superior expertise. Sure, I said. I would be a stewardess. I thought once a person landed a spot on a plane, she could work her way up to the cockpit. Groovy.

So I redirected my ambitions and decided to wear the spiffy uniform of flight attending. I geared up for a fascinating career of travel, adventure, and, surely, even- tually my own plane. But then I got measured. Back then, anyone who worked in the cabin had to be at least five foot two. And I was only five one—barely. Not to be deterred, I stood up straight; I hung from a door- way (someone told me I could stretch my spine that way); I teased my hair.

At the age of fifty-three, I semi-retired from teaching, and I started to feel that same itch to dream **big** and pursue new things.

Nothing worked. I stayed well below the minimum. Foiled.

I was depressed for a time. Walt Disney said—and I believed—that "if you can dream it, you can do it"; but no amount of dreaming could make me taller. After moping for a spell, I picked myself up and pursued careers without height requirements. I eventually found myself teaching college and training and consulting in the corporate arena—and loving it.

The story doesn't end there. At the age of fifty-three, I semi-retired from teaching, and I started to feel that same itch to dream big and pursue new things. And so I started writing romantic fiction. Under the pen name of E. K. Barber, I began to write the kind of books that I wanted to read. My heroine? An airline pilot. And a captain at that. And she's nearly six feet tall—ha. Walt Disney was right: if you can dream it, you really can do it. You just have to accommodate a few minor limitations.

There is considerable life after fifty. Whether you're yearning to write books or start a new career or get your ears pierced or see the Grand Canyon, life is full of all kinds of opportunities to color outside the lines. All it takes is a little dreaming.

Elaine Beaubien
Ruby RedHat's Ramblers,
Waterloo, Wisconsin

Brave at Any Age

My seventies were interesting, and fairly serene, but my eighties are passionate. I grow more intense as I age.

FLORIDA SCOTT-MAXWELL

You can't put an age on bravery. As her eightieth birthday approached, Norma Lamascus, who serves as queen mum of the Red and Purple R Us chapter of the Red Hat Society, made plans to celebrate in daredevil fashion: she decided to mark the occasion by jumping from a plane at twelve thousand feet, a stunt most twenty-five-year-olds haven't performed. "It's more fun than sitting in a rocking chair," she said. "Everyone should do it once." Her friends and family cheered after her safe landing, and photos were taken of her wearing a jump harness over a sweatshirt printed with "Red Hat Diva."

The CAMINO PILGRIMAGE

The first step binds one to the second.

FRENCH PROVERB

I'd been planning the trip for two years, and now it was time to embark on the journey. A TV spot about the hikers who walk the Santiago de Compostela Pilgrimage had piqued my attention a couple of years ago, and a friend gave me a guidebook from when she herself made the four-hundred-mile journey. Even though I read that only about 2 percent of all pilgrims were over the age of sixty, I knew I could do it—I had hiked all my life. And so, at the age of sixty-six, I set out on the pilgrimage often called "the Camino." I wanted to see the beautiful Spanish scenery, meet new and fascinating people, and accomplish a big goal.

The route I chose was the French route, beginning at the border of France and Spain at Roncesvalles. The trail winds 469 miles to the goal: the cathedral in Santiago de Compostela, where the remains of St. James the apostle are entombed.

Each year, over ninety countries from all over the world are represented on the trail. My fellow travelers and I spoke different languages and hiked at varying speeds, but we all wore the traditional shell on our packs to identify ourselves as pilgrims (or peregrinos or conchieros, as the pilgrims are called), and the same goal united all of us: to finish the route.

We stayed in alberques (or hostels) along the course, and sharing small spaces with these sojourners was surprisingly easy. Our exhaustion made sure we didn't chat too much—we just wanted to take showers (always cold) and find a place to eat to refuel our tired bodies. We came to expect a lack of toilet paper and soap, and we knew that anyone who came late to a full alberque would have to sleep on the floor.

The year I hiked was a holy year: each year that St. James Day, July 25, falls on a Sunday is designated a holy year, and all the pilgrims who journey to St. James's tomb are considered holy and inviolate. This means that helping the pilgrims is considered a special act, and so everyone we met in Spain was so gracious and helpful as we made our trek.

We rarely needed directions, though. We found that it was practically impossible to get lost on the Camino. Golden arrows and shells marked the entire route, even on detours for road construction. And so we made our way through northern Spain and wound through the small villages and a few large cities—Pamplona, Burgos, Leon. As we hiked, I grew to love Spain, its beauty and culture and the friendliness of the Spanish people.

> I felt the thrill of achieving a long sought-after goal, that moment when the accomplishment **finally** registers emotionally and you realize that you've achieved something you've never done before.

During the thirty-six days I took to complete the Pilgrimage, I was blessed in countless ways. I experienced the sparkling smiles and the generosity and hospitality of strangers. I felt the comfort of trusting my fellow travelers. I felt the thrill of communicating with someone in another language. I got to savor little blessings I so often take for granted: the fresh feeling after a much-needed shower; the smell of freshly mown hay, fresh flowers, and fine food. Best of all, I felt the thrill of achieving a long sought-after goal, that moment when the accomplishment finally registers emotionally and you realize that you've achieved something you've never done before.

I plan to make the journey again in a few years. This time, I want to take even longer. I want to go slow and have time to absorb and savor the culture of Spain. The rewards of the journey are many and will last a lifetime.

Kay Alderton
Divine Divas
Show Low, Arizona

A Marriage Made in Red Hat Heaven

To *succeed* *in life, you need*
three things: a wishbone,
a backbone and a *funnybone.*

REBA MCENTIRE

As far as anyone could tell, there had never been a Red Hat Society wedding, at least not in their area. Of course there had been reduations, coronations, and rites of passage galore, but to the best of anyone's knowledge, never a wedding. That changed one very special June when Robin Collier, a member of the Not-So-Prim Roses of Sneads Ferry, North Carolina, married Jeff Brown, her sweetheart of five years. Her Red Hat chaptermates planned the whole thing from top to bottom—Robin didn't even know the date of the wedding until the chapter told her.

When the groom saw his bride make her entrance, she was wearing a deep purple dress and a veil of red tulle. The groom and his best man wore black suits, purple shirts, red ties, and black cowboy hats. Purple and red feather boas climbed the lighted arch under which the couple stood as they read their vows, a fuzzy red heart hanging above them. Even the pastor who officiated wore red and purple.

When he pronounced them man and wife, the two exited under an arch of red hats held by Robin's chapter mates. After the ceremony, the two reminisced about the first time they met: a Halloween singles dance. ("I came as a rosebush—" Robin later shared. "And I wanted to pick some roses," Jeff jokingly interrupted.) They knew right away that what they both had in common was a love for fun and having a good time. So a Red Hat wedding only made sense for these two.

Life can bring us around a new corner at any time, in any stage. When it does, it calls for a celebration full of color and flair.

Robin Collier-Brown, Not-So-Prim Roses, Sneads Ferry, NC

BEHOLD *the* TURTLE

Old age is no place for sissies.

BETTE DAVIS

Several years ago, one of my teenage granddaughters, Jessica, informed me that she wanted to get a tattoo. I protested, "Oh, Jessica, don't get a tattoo on your beautiful body."

She answered without hesitation and with that spunk I loved so well, "I'm getting one, Grandma."

Clearly she wouldn't budge. It was time to pull out my most sensitive method of persuasion. So I said, "Jessie, wait until I am eighty-five, and then I will get a tattoo with you," not thinking I would ever make age eighty-five. She was delighted with the idea. My plan had worked.

Another year passed, and then another and another, and I was still going strong. And soon D-Day—the big eight-five—arrived on a sunny April morning. Jessica was at my door bright and early, ready to take me to the tattoo parlor. (Do they still call them "parlors"?)

What tattoo did I choose? I went with a discreet little turtle showing a perky attitude and wearing a red hat with a purple plume, patterned after my life motto: "Behold the turtle, who makes progress only when she sticks her neck out." I was definitely sticking my neck out that day, far from my comfort zone in the tattoo artist's chair.

And in the end, Jessica did not get a tattoo that day—my plucky little turtle came through for me just like I'd hoped.

Jewel Rogers
Brassy Brittany Babes,
St. Petersburg,
Florida

STARTING OVER

*Vitality shows in not only
the ability to persist but the
ability to start over.*

F. SCOTT FITZGERALD

The day after Christmas one winter, my husband and I lost everything in a house fire. Shocked and devastated, we began to pick up the pieces. Very slowly, we got on our feet again.

But even after we had settled in a new house and were back into our routines, for a long time I felt like the wind had left my sails. At work I often found myself staring at my computer—just staring, unable to do whatever I had sat down to do. As chief flight nurse for a busy air ambulance company and clinical supervisor of the entire medical crew, I was always on call. My responsibilities didn't leave me a day, or even a minute, really, to rest and recover from the stress of the job and from the stressors of life. I was getting more and more worn out, and I couldn't seem to get past the losses I'd experienced and the troubles and traumas I saw every day at work. I needed a change.

Soon an idea came to me, and it wouldn't quite let me go. I wanted to leave my high-stress job behind and open a little boutique, the kind of place where my friends and I would enjoy shopping and browsing. Every time I mentioned it, my husband looked at me like I was crazy, but that didn't stop me from researching small businesses and checking the paper for locations. I probably wouldn't actually *do* anything, I figured, but what was the harm in checking into it?

> I probably wouldn't **actually** *do* anything, I figured, but what was the harm in checking into it?

In the midst of my research efforts, I came to realize that I needed to take better care of myself. The stress was beginning to affect my health, and it had already affected my state of mind. So I quit my job. I just quit, without another offer or backup plan; I fully intended to do nothing for a while, take a sabbatical. It was time to take care of myself for a change.

About a week after turning in my thirty-day notice, I was browsing the Internet when I saw an ad for a little retail location. The price was about half of what I had seen in the past, and the building was located in a very desirable part of town, where all the tourists go. So, taking a chance, I contacted the leasing agent. "Before you tell me what you have in mind," she said, "let me tell you a little bit about the building where the shop is located."

She went on. "The shops in this building are all owned by women, and they all cater to women in the forty-five- to fifty-year-old range." Unbelievable! She asked what kind of store I wanted to open, and I told her that I'd long wanted to have a little store where ladies my age could gather and shop. There would be lots of fun clothes and accessories in my store, I told her, and lots of gadgets and novelties and pretty things.

She was amazed. "There have been eighteen other people interested in this shop, and I didn't feel good about any of them. But this sounds perfect!"

Ecstatic, I called a friend who had expressed an interest in opening a store with me. She got caught up in my excitement and said she had been praying for an opportunity to come along.

After signing about a million documents, we'll open our doors in two weeks, and everything in the shop looks great. I can't wait to see the faces that come through our doors.

I never thought I could be grateful for a house fire, but I have this feeling I never would have quit my job to go after my dream if I hadn't lost all that I did. Here I am, almost a year after losing everything I owned, doing something I'd been longing to do for years. My stress is gone, my anxiety has improved, and I'm feeling better than I have in a long time. There's a light at the end of this tunnel, and I've never been so excited about the future.

Lola Wipperman
The Sassy Sisters, San Diego, California

YOU'RE NEVER
Too OLD *to* PLAY

If you're **alive**, *you've got to flap*
your arms and legs, you've got to
jump around a lot, for **life** *is the very*
opposite of death, and therefore
you **must** *at very least think noisy*
and colorfully, or you're not alive.

MEL BROOKS

As a child, I was always playing make-believe, writing plays, creating characters and costumes. But as childhood faded away, so did my interest in playing dress-up. Life marched on with college, marriage, children, and a career teaching preschool, and my child-like creativity was buried under responsibilities.

Then one day, my aptly named friend Sherry Friend invited me to join the original chapter of the Red Hat Society. At first I was dubious about wearing a purple dress and a red hat to an outing with a group of similarly dressed women. It sounded peculiar. But I finally gave in and joined the chapter one fateful February.

When I did, I was introduced to a wonderful group of classy, fun-loving ladies. In the beginning, we were a bit fragmented because each of us brought in a new friend, and then we all had to get to know the new people. But just a few events later, we had become more than comfortable with our friendship, and we started looking forward to seeing each other more and more often.

Not only did I find sisterhood with the Red Hats, I also discovered all over again that I love to play. Getting creative with my Red Hat regalia and getting together with a group of women just for fun, nothing else, put me back in touch with my love for make-believe.

My new playtime often includes new personas. I have become Frieda Forlorno, a blonde who loves leopard-print anything (yes, I found purple leopard print); Rosie the Riveter, a factory worker; Becky Sue, a down-home Southern gal; and Ditsey Bomshelli, a Hollywood starlet wannabe. Oh, the things I have found in thrift stores, and oh, the fun I have had with them. Many of these eccentricities have materialized at conventions, and founder Sue Ellen Cooper has written about a few of them in her books.

> Not only did I find **sisterhood** with the Red Hats, I also discovered all over again that I love to play.

Yes, the Red Hat Society gave me terrific lifetime friends, and it also gave me an opportunity to play again. Play keeps our minds, spirits, and bodies thriving. It motivates us to socialize with our friends and helps us recognize our hidden talents, no matter our age.

When I took Sherry up on her offer to play, I had no idea that I would want to keep playing for the rest of my life. Fortunately, I have found the perfect playmates.

Sue Davis
The Fabulous Founders,
Fullerton, California

The BIRTHDAY

Forty is the old age of youth;
fifty is the youth of old age.

VICTOR HUGO

I'd heard about "Red Hat ladies," but I had no idea who they were or what they did. No one around me seemed to know why they dressed in red and purple or why there always seemed to be several of them clustered together. It was a mystery.

Then one day I was looking at an online discussion board for our small city, reading postings about the Red Hat ladies who had been spotted around town. A lot of people who posted seemed as confused as I was. But finally someone clued us in: Red Hat ladies were women age fifty and older who wore red hats and purple clothes and whose mission in life was to get together and have fun.

That sounded right up my alley. I love colorful clothes, and I love to have a good time. There was a problem, of course: I wasn't yet fifty. And this left me feeling deeply disappointed.

This was the first time in my life that I thought about turning fifty with hope and anticipation, the way a little girl waits for her birthday party, instead of dread. I had always thought of that particular birthday as a half-century milestone, which sounded miserable. Now I'd found something good about turning fifty, and it made the birthday seem much farther away than I wanted it to be.

My curiosity hadn't quite been sated; I was still dying to know more about these Red Hat ladies. So I went to my computer and typed "red hat ladies" into a search engine. The first link on the results list took me to the Red Hat Society Web site, and there I read about how the organization—or, excuse me, *dis*organization—began and what they did. I clicked my way to their online store and admired all the pretty things. I felt like I was in heaven as I eyed the reds and purples and pinks and lavenders, although I didn't yet know what the pinks and lavenders signified.

After a little more clicking, I found information about how to start a chapter. I wanted to be ready to get started as soon as I hit the big five-oh. And that's when I discovered that until I turned fifty, I could be a Pink Hatter and wear the lavender and pink rather than purple and red—and I could also start my own chapter as a Pink Hatter.

I didn't waste a minute. I enlisted my sister as my first potential member. My daughter was next. She resisted at first, but she finally gave in, saying she was so stressed that she could use some fun time. At our first little meeting, we got together to swap ideas and plans, and then and there the Rosebuds and Petals chapter of the Red Hat Society was born. My sister came up with the name. "Petals" represents the Red Hatters, while "Rosebuds" represents us Pink Hatters.

It wasn't long before we became an official chapter of six royal subjects who just want to have fun. I wrote a pledge and held an induction ceremony, complete with membership cards and certificates. And that's where the fun began.

For most of our meetings, we get together at a park and have a picnic, talking, laughing, dancing (our chapter's theme dance is the chicken dance), and just being together. Sometimes we go shopping and try to find good bargains and craft ideas. Sometimes—most of the time—we eat.

For one of our "dress-ups" (our word for "meetings"), I purchased a pack of toy teeth made to look as though they hadn't been brushed in a few years. Each of us put a set of the teeth in our mouths, and now I have some classic shots for our scrapbook.

> This was the first time in my life that I thought about turning fifty with hope and anticipation, the way a little girl waits for her birthday party, instead of dread.

Our chapter has a Komplaint Keeper, a Voter Toter, a Cash Calculator, and a Scribbling Scriptor. We also have a few designated "worry warts." If any of our members are troubled by something, they can enlist a worry wart to help them worry about it for a week. We find it helps to know that someone else is worrying with us. Rosebuds and Petals also has a mascot, a life-size soft sculpt doll named Minnie Pausal. Her red hat has a flower for each member's birth month, and she rides in the car with me to our dress-ups.

In just a few months, I will have "the birthday"—and I can't wait. I know that when I trade in my pink hat for a red one, our chapter will have even more fun (if that's possible). There will be even more chances to let loose, forget our troubles, and just laugh, and we'll make new friends, learn new things, and try things we never would have thought ourselves capable of. That half-century milestone is looking better and better.

Connie C. Smith

Rosebuds and Petals,
Crossville,
Tennessee

A VERY SPECIAL REDUATION

There is nothing quite so deeply satisfying as the solidarity of a family united across the generations and miles by a common faith and history.

SARA WENGER SHENK

Ever since Sue Ellen Cooper gave me a red hat ten years ago, I've had the good fortune to attend many Red Hat events among chapters of all sizes, with Red and Pink Hatters of all ages, and in many parts of the United States and Canada. I like to call these gatherings "giggles," because anytime we get together, lots of giggles are invariably heard.

I've also had the pleasure of witnessing or even presiding over several reduations, those wonderful ceremonies we share on the advent of a member's fiftieth birthday. Each is a special time of expectant celebration, and often hilarity, as a Pink Hatter comes of age and has her pink hat replaced with one of red. We Red Hatters like to say, "Now you're ready to play with the big girls!"

On one of these special occasions, it was a dear friend of mine, Sue, who was nearing the magical birthday. The date coincided nicely with a trip my husband and I had planned to upstate New York, where Sue and her husband lived. I had always hoped to be able to reduate her; I'd even chosen a red hat a whole year before just for the occasion. Now the hat would get to make an appearance.

The honoree was alerted, invitations extended, and plans finalized for a small giggle to gather on the patio of a lovely restaurant overlooking Canandaigua Lake. Oh, what a giggle it was. We represented five decades—or seven, if you consider that Sue was a few days shy of her fiftieth birthday and thus bridged the forties and fifties, and as Doris, at age 101, put it, "I have already lived through my nineties and should be able to claim that decade too, don't you think?"

"Of course," we responded in chorus.

There we were in full regalia: two in their fifties, two in their sixties, two in their seventies, one in her eighties, and Doris, 101. This giggle also happened to include my mother, and Doris whispered to me, "I was in college before your mother was born."

Sue's mother, also in attendance, added, "Sue wasn't even born when Doris could have become a Red Hatter, if there had been such a thing fifty-one years ago."

Two Red Hat chapter queens in the giggle offered a toast to our honoree, and we clinked glasses with much aplomb. Then we joined hands around Sue and officially reduated her. I lifted her pink hat, and a wide-brimmed red one took its place. We draped a purple shawl around her shoulders, and Sue blushed a bit as other patrons captured the moment on our cameras—and theirs.

I think I'll always remember that particular giggle. We shared many stories and much love that day, generations of women linked arm in arm.

Linda Murphy
The Fabulous Founders,
Fullerton, California,
and the Steel Magnolias,
Homosassa, Florida

The LIFE IN YOUR YEARS

In youth we learn;
in age we **understand.**

MARIE VON EBNER-ESCHENBACH

I watched as the ball arced over the net in my direction. This shot would be mine. I would show these "old ladies" what they were up against. I was twenty-five and they were easily twice that, and there was no way I was going to lose the point.

I moved into position, ready to spike the ball to victory, or at least over the net. I shouted, "I've got it!" and a voice yelled right next to my ear, "No you don't, honey!" In the next instant, I felt my shirt rip down my back, taking a bit of skin along with it, and I was flung face first into the net. I bounced back like a rag doll and landed on my back, winded.

"The point's no good—she touched the net!" yelled a member of the other team. Dazed, I looked up to see my future mother-in-law, Helen. "Mildred doesn't like it when someone gets in her way. I hope she didn't hurt you." She offered me her hand. My pride was wounded more than my scratched back, which burned like fire ants dancing along my spine. "No, I'm fine. Really." I knew my face was bright red, and tears were stinging my eyes, but I got up, walked over to Mildred, and apologized for screwing up the point. She gave a small shrug, muttering, "Well, that was the winning point, you know." She paused and looked me in the eye. "But since you're Helen's new daughter-in-law—almost—and her guest, we'll let it go. You're young and inexperienced." Ah, the crowning blow: "young and inexperienced." How dare she.

After the volleyball game, we all went to the pool to do some cool-down laps. Here I managed to out lap at least some of the women as I pulled from my small remaining reserve of strength and gave it all I had. As I look back now, it seems highly possible that one or two let me win. They probably smiled inwardly at my youthful arrogance and forgave me, knowing, or perhaps hoping, that I would pick up some wisdom of my own down the road of life.

They probably smiled inwardly at my youthful arrogance and forgave me, knowing, or perhaps hoping, that I would pick up some wisdom of my own down the road of life.

That was more than thirty years ago. Next year I turn sixty (an age I could not even comprehend when I was twenty-five) and I look with new understanding at these approaching golden years and back at those days when I thought I was invincible. I've come face-to-face with my human frailty on many occasions over the years; I've come to realize that those women knew a lot more than I did about living life for all it was worth.

Helen is still vibrant and energetic in her mid-eighties. She exercises, swims, travels, and tends her garden. Her skin would be the envy of many half her age. When I find myself groaning as I get out of bed in the morning or whining because my tennis arm isn't what it used to be, I remind myself that these little hang-ups are just part of the circle of life, and I think of my amazing mother-in-law and those gutsy women of thirty years ago. As Helen would say, "If you want to keep those joints lubricated, you have to move the parts."

Smiling at the memory, I get myself out the door to hike or exercise or dance. I surround myself with a sisterhood of energetic women just like Helen, and we laugh, eat chocolate, and do the twist. We are grandmothers setting new standards for senior citizens—in fact, we are setting all the old guidelines on their ears.

No Geritol for this granny, although I might need a little joint cream after a tough game of volleyball. I do have to keep up with Helen, after all, and that is no easy task.

Linda Leary
La Fleur Rouge
Loveland,
Colorado

I'm TOO YOUNG to BE OLD

You can't help getting older,

but you don't have to get old.

GEORGE BURNS

I believe that at some point we consciously decide that we are old. I remember this exact moment in my life. I massaged the arthritis pain in my shoulder and knee, and all of sudden I fully recognized that various body parts were dropping or drooping, that gray hair had made a stunning appearance. I was old.

Oh, well, I told myself. *This is what happens if you live long enough. It's inevitable.* I thought about the old people I knew when I was a little girl, how they looked, how they smelled. Now I was one of them. I now knew that one of the smells was ointment for arthritis. And now I knew why they said, "I can't do that . . . I can't go . . . my arthritis, my lumbago." (Whatever happened to lumbago, anyway? Does no one get it anymore?)

I was old for about two months. One day, as I was deciding who would receive my high heels and who would drive me on errands, it hit me: I was too young to be old. I would do my own driving. I would continue traveling—and wearing high heels. There was a lot more I wanted to say, and I was going to keep talking, keep making the world take notice.

Whew, I thought. *That was a close call. Almost got old there for a minute.*

I realized that if we think we are old, then we are. Who was I to mope about my advancing years? I was living in the best of times to be a senior. They made arthritis medicines that didn't smell. There were all kinds of solutions for dropping and drooping body parts. There were beautiful shoes with arch support. Wasn't seventy the new fifty?

> I was old for about two months. One day, as I was deciding who would receive my high heels and who would drive me on errands, it hit me: I was too young to be old.

I read Psalm 92:14: "They shall still bear fruit in old age; they shall be fresh and flourishing" (NKJV). This made me think about our spirit, how the spirit we have in old age is the same spirit we had when we were young. Our bodies may age, but our spirit doesn't have to. It can grow wiser and stronger and better.

Thinking about this made me realize that just because we are seniors doesn't mean we have nothing left to offer: we have the benefit of age and experience. I think we should consciously remember to put our shoulders back with pride. We should put some pep in our step and some glide in our stride. We should keep on living, and we should enjoy life even more than we did when we were young. We have miles to go before we sleep. I remember a quote I heard long ago, attributed to George Eliot: "It's never too late to be what you might have become." As I thought about growing older, I realized that I had the power to make my senior years the richest and fullest of my life.

There are new chapters in my life just waiting for me to write them. I'm planning new adventures and scheming to have fun in all kinds of ways. And I'm convinced that the best is yet to come.

Claudreen Jackson

*Scarlet Sophistication,
West Bloomfield,
Michigan*

CONFESSIONS
of a RELUCTANT RED HATTER

*It takes a long **time** to become young.*

PABLO PICASSO

Becoming a member of the Red Hat Society had no appeal for me. Sitting around with a bunch of old ladies? No way. Okay, so I definitely met the age requirement. But I didn't look it, act it, think it, or feel it. However, when "1937" appears anywhere on your birth certificate, there's no denying that you're a senior citizen. You have senior moments (I hate that phrase), and you take advantage—discreetly, mind you—of senior citizens' discounts (I love that phrase).

"I'll try it once," I grumbled to my friend, who was gung-ho about joining a chapter. "But don't expect me to go a second time." I bought the cheapest red hat I could find and an equally cheap purple scarf to tie around the brim, because I knew I'd toss them after the first get-together. I wore a lot of red and purple anyway (though not usually together, of course), so other than buying a hat, I didn't need to shop for new clothes. Red shoes, check. Red handbag, check. I even had red and purple jewelry. I definitely looked the part, even if I was only going to a meeting just this once.

My friend had talked a couple of other friends into going with us to our first luncheon, and I was still grumbling a little as we arrived. I would *not* have a good time today. I was sure of it.

But even though I certainly didn't intend to, I loved it. We all did. Here I sat with a wonderful bunch of women, much cooler chicks than I had expected. They were friendly, outgoing, and interesting. We sat with a retired college professor, a small business owner, and a grandmother who came to the luncheon on her motorcycle. (I hyperventilate on any bike without training wheels, so I was in awe of her.) And when it came time to pay our dues, vote for a name for our chapter, and sign up for the next luncheon, I whipped out my wallet, wrote out my vote for our chapter name, and put my name on the luncheon roster for the next month.

Although we're from the Niskayuna area of Schenectady, we ended up joining the Clifton Park group (just a short jog up I-87) because our friend who initially got us interested in the Red Hats was then living near Clifton Park. Two other women from

> Here I sat with a wonderful bunch of women, much cooler chicks than I had expected. They were friendly, outgoing, and interesting.

Niskayuna recently joined our group. They met our queen mum at a fashion show function one day, and she invited them to one of our luncheons. They accepted the invite and quickly fell in love with our group. The next time they came, they sat with my friends and me, and we quickly became Niskayuna friends. And, as they say, the rest is all red and purple.

Whether e-mailing each other, chatting on the phone, or sharing tidbits and updates in person, these new friends and I are experiencing a whole new world. These women are fun, sometimes naughty, but always nice. They revive me, stimulate me, and energize me. We laugh together and sometimes have serious conversations too. We support, commiserate with, and encourage each other anytime support, commiseration, or encouragement is needed. I feel rewarded to be part of the wonderful camaraderie of these "with it" ladies who come from such diverse backgrounds.

Me, a Red Hatter? You better believe it. Admitting that I'm over sixty? Ditto. Age is just a number, and spending time with Red Hat friends has given me a new outlook on growing older with my new BFF (best friends forever). Together, we make sixty look cool.

Lynn Paska
The Red Hat Mamas,
Clifton Park,
New York

A Wild Welcome

In the end, it's not
the years in your life that count.
It's the life in your years.

ABRAHAM LINCOLN

We'd heard the stories other chapters told of their
reduations, and we couldn't wait to have one of our
own. Since we only had one Pink Hatter, we knew we
had to make her reduation as much fun as possible.
And so, as her birthday approached, we set to work.

When we booked the restaurant, we thought we had
reserved a dining room to ourselves. When we arrived,
however, we found that we had been seated in the
general dining room. But that wasn't about to stop us
from being as crazy as we wanted to be.

As soon as the reduate, Denise, arrived in her brassy
pink and lavender, the fun could begin. Everyone in the
restaurant was enthralled by us, as if they sensed that
something big was about to happen. As the reduation
got underway, two small children sitting nearby couldn't
stop staring; they even clapped every time we all did

something. And two senior couples across from our table turned their chairs around so they could have ring-side seats. Of course we gave them a good show.

First, we had Denise affirm our chapter's code of conduct:

Are you ready to leave behind your "pinkness" and move forward to embrace and enjoy the spirit of the Sassy Scarlet Sirens?

Will you proudly wear your RHS colors?

Will you laugh often, loud, and long? Laugh until you gasp for air?

Will you use these gatherings as an excuse to dress in flamboyant attire?

Do you approve wholeheartedly of our motto: "Fun for all, and all for fun"?

Will you keep talk at our gatherings light, happy, or funny?

She said, "I will," to all of our requests, and then we all blew out a pink candle on the table. One of the ladies lit a red candle sitting beside it, and I read the rest of the reduation "liturgy":

"Your sisters have put out your pink candle's flame. In its place we offer this candle of red to hold as we place a red hat on your head. So listen closely, my sisters fair, 'cause we haven't got a minute to spare. This princess has made her last pink bow, and she's aching to be a Red Hatter now!

"No longer is fifty a birthday to dread, but cause for a celebration instead. And so we salute a former Pink Hatter as we proudly proclaim that Red Hatters matter! Now gather ye round and join hand in hand, and ask that our sister, Denise, please stand, as I carefully lift her pink hat from her head, to replace it today with a chapeau in red! We shall also drape purple over her shoulder, the color we wear as we grow older."

Then the ladies removed her pink hat and placed a red graduation cap on her head, draping her in a sequined purple shawl. I announced proudly: "Reduation's complete, so we announce this day that Denise is now

Everyone in the restaurant was **enthralled** *by us, as if they sensed that something big was about to happen. Of course we gave them a good show.*

ready to come out with the big girls and play. Congratulations and welcome to the red league of the Sassy Scarlet Sirens!" And with smiles and hugs, everyone cheered and gave Denise a red rose.

The restaurant staff also joined in the laughter and fun, chatting with us and clapping at the end of our ceremony. And a local newspaper reporter stopped by our table to wish us well and say that in all her years of reporting, she had never seen anything quite like our special ritual. (Of course not.)

One of the senior ladies seated nearby also came by our table to talk. She asked if I'd e-mail her a copy of the poem "Warning" and said she would be looking for a chapter near her hometown. Before today, she hadn't realized our group had so much fun.

My granddaughter Skyler is our unofficial mascot, and a Pink Hatter at nine years old. When our reduation drew to a close, I quipped, "Well, we only have to wait forty-one years to do one for Skyler!" Everyone cheered. They couldn't wait.

Elaine Kooker
Sassy Scarlet Sirens,
Quakertown, Pennsylvania

Stages in Life

When I was a child,
They did not call me difficult,
Nor did they call me a wild child.
They said I was
A free spirit.

When I was a young adult,
They did not say I was gullible,
A dingbat or a space cadet.
They said I was
Unique.

And now—
As I enjoy the privileges of
Being a senior citizen—
They do not call me that crazy old lady.
No, no! I have become
Eccentric.

DONNA M. GRAY
VIRGINIA BEACH DARLIN' DIVAS, VIRGINIA BEACH, VIRGINIA

A WEDDING *to* REMEMBER

*There is no more lovely,
friendly, and charming relationship,
communion, or company
than a good marriage.*

MARTIN LUTHER

One February day I was listening to a country music radio station, when I heard an announcement for a contest they were holding. Engaged and married couples could enter, and on the Sunday before Valentine's Day, the winning couples would be wed or renew their vows in the lawn and garden center of a nearby Wal-Mart.

I gasped and turned up the radio. My husband and I had recently been talking about renewing our vows in celebration of our fiftieth anniversary. The milestone meant a lot to us, and we wanted to do the celebration up big. Our wedding had been a very practical affair. My husband came home from the air force on a three-day pass, and we quickly found a minister and got married. No flowers or cake or bridesmaids, just a simple ceremony and a few family members. Married fifty years and still going strong, we wanted our renewal ceremony to be sweet and memorable with a little flair—just like our marriage.

This contest sounded like it might be just what we needed. So I entered, and we were chosen. My friend and the queen mother of my Red Hat Society chapter, Margo, was a wedding planner by trade, and she got to work organizing everything for that special Sunday. She made me a beautiful bridal bouquet of red, purple, and white silk flowers, and my fellow Sweet Magnolias were invited to serve as bridesmaids. I wore a purple hat and veil and a red dress, while the bridesmaids wore purple with red hats. What a colorful group my wedding party made! We were definitely noticeable against all the black suits and white satin dresses.

Four couples were wed for the first time, and eight renewed their vows. After the ceremony, the organizers held a drawing for prizes donated by local merchants. My lucky husband and I won the drawing, and we received new gold wedding bands and a gift

Married fifty years and still going strong, we wanted our renewal ceremony to be sweet and memorable with a little flair—just like our marriage. This contest sounded like it might be just what we needed.

basket filled with bubbly brew, strawberries, chocolates, and a gift card for a year's supply of Krispy Kreme doughnuts.

As the winners of the drawing, my husband and I had the first dance. We were also presented with a beautiful three-tier wedding cake, which I cut and served to the more than one hundred people in attendance. As the day drew to a close, one of my attending grandsons piped up in his little voice, "Me-Ma, this was a hoot!" He was right. This fun-filled ceremony was a colorful and unforgettable moment, such a perfect celebration of what had begun with a simple ceremony fifty years earlier. I felt just like Cinderella. And you're never too old to be Cinderella.

June Griggs
The Sweet Magnolias,
Charleston,
South Carolina

HEARTS OF GOLD

By the time we hit our fifties, we've weathered a storm or two. And the tragedies we've survived have a way of softening our hearts toward others. We know we're all in this together, and we know that what we do matters, whether it's a random act of kindness or a habit of caring for those close to us. Our compassion is just another quality that makes us true gems, jewels that shine even when the light is dim.

Kind and caring

HAND-ME-DOWN
Fun

*Those who bring sunshine
to the lives of others
cannot keep it from themselves.*

JAMES MATTHEW BARRIE

My Red Hat chapter, the Gadabout Gals, recently enjoyed a wonderful Saturday afternoon with a reuses sale of our Red Hat finery—dresses, jewelry, and of course plenty of hats. When all of us cleaned out our closets, the living room sale that resulted was quite an upscale resale shop. And by the end of the day, we had all found many treasured bargains. But there was still quite an inventory of items remaining.

I didn't especially want to take any of my items back home, so I wondered if I could donate everything to a thrift store or senior center. When I pitched this idea to the other ladies, they enthusiastically and generously agreed, and I left with a bag full of hats and a plastic tote full of clothes.

Now all I had to do was find a place to donate this fine merchandise. My mother's assisted living center might be interested, I thought. She had loved the idea of the Red Hat Society and once attended a tea with me. But since she passed away last Christmas, I found it difficult to visit the facility where she had lived—it was far away and held a few too many memories. So I made mental plans to call a senior center in my neighborhood the following week. But God had other ideas.

On Monday morning, I received a call from none other than my mom's assisted living center. Their financial office had overlooked a small personal account I kept for my mom and wanted to send it to me right away. As we talked, I decided to see if their activities director might be interested in our Red Hat donations, so I asked for her office. Since she was unavailable, I left a message.

A short time later, I received a return call from a breathless woman named Angel, who seemed thrilled that I had called—our donations would be more than welcome. She had promised the women residents that they would start a Red Hat group and had been trying to find a way to keep her promise.

> She was **overwhelmed** by the generosity of the Gadabout Gals. We both felt that we were watching God at work.

Her voice was rich with emotion as she explained that the ladies in her care didn't have extra money to buy hats and dresses, and she had been at a loss for a solution to their dilemma. She'd remained optimistic about the situation, though; she was just sure her prayers would be answered. The serendipitous donation of hats and dresses was just what she'd prayed for. We both felt that we were watching God at work, and I knew my mother would have loved to see this unexpected little blessing.

The very next day, my husband and I delivered all the goodies. I included a note with our queen mum's address, and a few days later she received a wonderful letter of appreciation. We're in talks to coordinate an event at the new chapter's location soon.

I can't wait to see these ladies in their new, yet familiar, red hats, to meet a whole new group of sisters intent on sharing laughter and fun.

Mary Ann Winters
The Gadabout Gals,
Galena, Ohio

A Helping Hand

Shared joy is a double joy;
shared sorrow is half a sorrow.

SWEDISH PROVERB

Not too long ago, a member of Central Oregon's Classy RH Ladies of Madras received word that her forty-seven-year-old son had been diagnosed with stage four Hodgkins lymphoma. She had no resources to get to Vermont from Oregon. So the chapter's vice mother called each of the twenty members, and within a few hours the group had collected enough money for her airline ticket and all other expenses. One member shared the story with her sister in Texas, who donated all of her airline miles to help.

In the fun times and the hard times, everyone needs a group of loving, caring friends who can play together as well as stand strong together in all of life's circumstances.

Donna DeWhitt
Classy Red Hat Ladies, Madras, Oregon

THROUGH THICK
and THIN

In everyone's life, at some time,
our *inner fire* goes out.
It is then burst into flame
by an *encounter* with
another human being.
We should all be thankful
for those people who *rekindle*
the inner *spirit*.

ALBERT SCHWEITZER

As we get older, life gets more . . . complicated. Sure, there are grandkids to spoil and cake to be eaten and fun to be had. But you don't get to be our age without seeing a few tough days along the way.

Last March, our chapter, located in a retirement community lost a new member very unexpectedly. Judy had just taken over the chair of the pot luck committee, and one night she didn't show up to help set up the hall or even attend the dinner. No one was able to reach her. And then we learned that she had had some recent heart health concerns, and that she had passed away in her sleep.

Several of us ladies sprang into action, led by the chairwoman of our sunshine committee, to help the family with the memorial arrangements. About a dozen of us attended the funeral, and one of us gave a eulogy for our lost sister.

After the services, family and friends gathered in our community clubhouse. We set up a specially decorated food table, and we all prepared food. The family stopped by and murmured their thanks

> **You don't get to be our age without seeing a few tough days along the way.**

with looks of surprise; I don't think they'd ever seen such a display of dedication from virtual strangers. Their gratitude touched us, and we were all very happy to be able to help them and honor Judy in the style that any friend of ours deserves.

Later that fall, a chapter member suffered the unexpected loss of her only son at the young age of thirty. Again we all joined together to comfort Kathy and help our sister get through this tragedy.

I can't quite describe the compassion and love that each one of us feels for our sisters during difficult times. We have learned that there is nothing we can't endure as long as we support and take care of each other. At our age, we are bound to experience a loss, and we did. We are bound to experience a host of health problems, affecting ourselves or our loved ones, and we have. We spend time together. We pray a lot. We know that someone is always there with us to help us cope. In spite of all our trials and tribulations, we still enjoy each day to the fullest and choose to have lots of fun, helping each other along the way.

Shirley Riscile
Riverside Rascals,
Ruskin, Florida

The Best Medicine

Mirth is God's medicine.
Everybody ought to bathe in it.

HENRY WARD BEECHER

The last several weeks had tried all of our spirits. My aunt had battled multiple myeloma, a treatable kind of blood cancer, for twelve years now, and over time it had weakened her immune system. She had recently caught pneumonia, and then the pneumonia decided to settle in her artificial hip, causing a nasty infection.

Because her body had begun to reject the prosthesis, the doctors removed her artificial hip, and then the next day they operated again to deliberately break her femur in order to get the antibiotics into her bones. They could not give her a new hip for another six weeks to be certain that the infection had completely cleared. So she spent lots of time in a hospital bed with no right hip and a broken femur. One day they even got her out of bed to teach her how to walk with a walker without putting any weight on her right hip.

My relatives and I were amazed at all she had endured. As often happens in my family (I must come from sturdy stock), she had rebounded so well from the infection that the doctors thought they could send her home soon. But she would have a tough road ahead of her even after she returned home.

My entire family brought all kinds of things to the hospital to help her endure her stay. Flowers, candy, magazines, books, and movies filled her room. But I wanted to bring her something different. I wanted to bring something out of the ordinary, something that would make her laugh with surprise.

So one day my mom and I arrived at the hospital with a bag full of goodies. We walked into her room and said hi to my aunt. "Well, I brought you a few little somethings—just a few things I really hope you enjoy," I told my aunt, suddenly feeling a little shy, and she looked at me tiredly, but with expectation.

She grabbed my hand and told me that she hadn't laughed that hard in a long time and that she loved her gifts. "That kazoo is priceless!"

The first thing I pulled out of the bag was a red kazoo on a red lanyard. I put it around her neck, and she got tickled with laughter, saying, "I didn't even know they still made these!" She played a few bars from a few indistinguishable songs, and I smiled.

Next came a pair of bright red wax lips, and then she started laughing really hard. "I didn't know they still made these either! My word. I can't wait to wear these the next time the nurses come in. Won't they be surprised!"

To top it all off, I had brought her a fancy red hat trimmed to the brim with braiding, silk flowers, and feathers. I pulled it out of my bag and said, "Nobody can be 'blue' in a red hat, right? So anytime you get to feeling sad, you can just put this on, and you'll be feeling better in no time."

She put it on her head and smiled. "I think you're right," she said.

I visited for a while longer with her and my mom, and then I got ready to leave. Before I left, she grabbed my hand and told me that she hadn't laughed that hard in a long time and that she loved her gifts. "That kazoo is priceless! I'm going to have so much fun with this stuff."

My mom walked out with me. "That was such a good idea!" she told me. "You really made her day." I'd come to the hospital with the goal of making her laugh, and it looked like I'd succeeded.

It seemed that those three little items worked a little magic that day. Laughter is healing for the body and soul, and I think a little dose of whimsy and fun was just what she needed to keep up her strength. Never underestimate the power of a sassy hat.

Deb Zimmerman
Diva Dolls, Hicksville, Ohio

A DAY at the RACES

If I had to sum up Friendship

in one word, it would be Comfort.

ADABELLA RADICI

Sometimes real life seems like something out of a TV movie. I know I've seen some strange days. You never know when life will bring you a little bit of laughter or a little bit of trouble, sometimes both in the same day.

Recently my eighty-one-year-old father was diagnosed with colon cancer. The doctors' words shook me; I took the news harder than when I learned of my own cancer. I told him of the diagnosis on a Monday, we saw the surgeon on Tuesday, Dad went in for a CAT scan on Wednesday, and we spent the rest of the week at doctors' appointments or visiting the clinic. It was good that everything was happening quickly—the sooner the better for my dad's health—but it also made for a difficult week. Even with neighbors, friends, and family offering their support, I still wilted under the high concentration of stressful events.

I guess the stress contributed to my oversleeping on the morning of his surgery. We were scheduled for an 8:45 a.m. surgery and were to check in at 6:45. Dad and Mom knocked at my door at 6:05, and I was still in bed. I let them in, ran through the shower, made my face, dressed, and then drove the twenty-minute course to the hospital. We arrived with no time to spare.

We shakily kissed Dad good-bye before they wheeled him down the hall, and then we turned the corner to go into the surgical waiting area. What I saw next made me jump a little, then smile tearfully: my entire Red Hat group appeared before me in full regalia. My sisters strutted their gorgeous selves in purple adorned with fur and feather boas, and pins in the shape of horses whinnied on brims of their hats. They were headed for an outing at the horse races and had come to the hospital first to give me moral support.

We shakily kissed Dad good-bye before they wheeled him down the hall, and then we turned the corner to go into the surgical waiting area. What I saw next made me jump a little, then smile tearfully.

Their glorious colors were a delight to my spirit on that trying day. Even better, their love, encouragement, and well wishes (plus all their prayers) gave me that little boost I knew I would need. They were seven angels in purple and red.

These spirited gals have hearts of gold—or maybe diamonds. Whatever they're made of, it's something that sparkles and is very precious.

Dianne Luebbert
Kentucky Red Hat
Boa Babes,
Henderson, Kentucky

LAUGH LINES

We've spent years making other people happy, and now it's our turn to have a good time. And have a good time we will—no one knows more about fun than we do. Whether it's a lavish lunch or a simple tea, a wild party or a long laugh at something seemingly insignificant, we're experts in the art of making life fun. These next few stories might give you a few ideas for a crazy soiree of your own, or they might just give you something to smirk about. Either way, don't be afraid to laugh it up: our laugh lines are what make us fabulous. *A good time*

A NEW GAME PLAN

Laughter is the shortest distance between two people.

VICTOR BORGE

I was a typical mom, I suppose. From the time my boys were born until they graduated from high school, their schedule was my schedule, from Little League to football practice to student council meetings to proms. I started each day by checking their schedules to see who needed to be where and at what time.

I wouldn't have wanted to miss a minute of those years. And as the boys moved on and moved out, I had a few adjustments to make. To my surprise, though, I realized one day that it wasn't only them that I missed. Of course I missed that everyday contact with my kids, but I also missed hanging out with other sports moms at practices and games. We no longer saw each other, and we'd lost contact.

The day I realized I had a planner and could write my own schedule was quite a day of discovery. The problem was that my weeks looked so bare. My husband and I planned a few fun things just for us, but I still missed that friendship with other women.

About the same time that I came to this realization, I happened to see an article in the newspaper about a local chapter of the Red Hat Society. They had a smorgasbord of activities planned and were accepting new members. It sounded like just what I'd been missing—friendship, new places to visit, and dinner out once a month.

The article gave the number of the queen mother, and I marked it with my finger on the inky newsprint as I dialed. The voice on the other end cheerily told me to come by her shop to register. Sounds like a plan, I told her.

But when I walked into her store, I wondered if I had made a mistake. Her shop was a dainty boutique, and she herself looked refined and delicate. I, on the other hand, have always been a bit of a country girl, and I usually wear clothes I can throw straight into the washer. If all the ladies in the group were like their leader, I was sure I would not fit in. I looked down at the knees of my sturdy jeans self-consciously.

She'd already greeted me, so I couldn't just walk away. "I came to register for your Red Hat Society chapter," I said, then added, "but I've been thinking I might wait a while."

Her friendliness and excitement completely overtook my sudden shyness. She acted as if she'd known me all her life, and her bubbly personality put me at ease right away. So I signed up—and also signed up my sister and my best friend.

She told me where to show up for their next gathering, and I bought a boa from the boutique. Giggling all the way to my car, I hopped inside and called my sister and my friend. "Mark your calendars!" I told them. "We're going to a Red Hat party!"

A few weeks later, my friend and I drove to the restaurant, and in the parking lot we put on our red hats for the first time. We laughed so hard, we knew we'd officially been bitten by the Red Hat bug.

Since that time, we've rarely missed a get-together. (My sister still has a rigorous schedule with her kids, so she wasn't able to stay on with the chapter. But just give her a few years—she'll be a Red Hatter for sure.) We've gone places and tried things I never would have thought of on my own, and we've connected with a whole network of women who seem to want the same thing we want: a group of friends with whom to laugh and spend time and have fun.

We laugh a lot, pass around plenty of photos of grandchildren, play dress up, and eat scrumptious desserts. We also share each other's successes and struggles. I have a twenty-nine-year-old son who is severely handicapped and lives at home with us. I wouldn't have it any other way, but of course there are struggles, and my Red Hat friends have a special way of listening to me and giving me new courage and energy. They can turn a bad day around like no one I've ever met; we have a blast together.

Thanks to my newfound sisters, my planner is full of activities— and my life is full of laughter and fun.

Patricia Knicely
Valley Girls, McGraheysville, Virginia

AIN'T MISBEHAVIN'

People are more fun than anybody.

DOROTHY PARKER

After asking the mayor of our small town if he would officially proclaim April 25 Red Hat Day and receiving his consent, our chapter visited his office to have our picture taken with him for our local newspaper. During our visit, he asked if we would like to lead the Pledge of Allegiance before a city council meeting sometime, and we delightedly agreed. We set a date right then and there.

On that special evening, we donned our red hats and purple regalia and ascended the stairs to the council's chambers. We had a great time greeting friends, meeting local statesmen, and of course leading the group in pledging allegiance to the flag of our great nation.

Afterward four of us sat on the stone benches outside city hall talking, laughing, and having an all around good time. I suppose we got a little loud, and as the cars passed, several drivers tooted their horns and waved.

We were still enjoying the night air and the conversation when a young lady exited a restaurant across the street. She stopped at her car directly in front of us and waved.

> Who would have thought that four upstanding citizens, who helped lead civic events, would be suspected of soliciting?

"I just wanted to tell you all something amusing. I just finished a business dinner—my company is entertaining a client from Africa. When he came into the restaurant, he said, 'Are those ladies across the street soliciting?' I wasn't sure I'd heard him right, so I asked him to repeat the question, and he said, 'Are those ladies over there soliciting? In Africa when we see women on a street corner wearing bright colors such as they have on, they are usually soliciting.'"

When we heard this, the four of us laughed so hard we had to hold on to our knees, and I'm fairly certain we grew loud enough to attract even more attention. The young lady smiled and told us to enjoy the rest of our evening, and we waved our good-bye, still laughing. Who would have thought that four upstanding citizens, who helped lead civic events, would be suspected of soliciting?

That's one of the best things about the wearing of the red hat: whenever we get together in public, we get noticed.

Phyllis Grant
Red Hats Go 4 Fun,
Statesville, North Carolina

It Doesn't Take Much

Fun is about as good a habit as there is.

JIMMY BUFFETT

At our monthly chapter luncheon, my fellow Red Hatters and I were having a little fun at a restaurant. I, Queen Brenda Foo Foo, was demonstrating the use of my new cell phone and the music I'd chosen as a ring tone. (It doesn't take much to entertain us, really.) Royal Mother Ram, known to outsiders as Deb Lewis, was fascinated by the idea that I had actual music on my phone rather than just beeps and two-tone rings, and she began to dance. Of course I couldn't let her dance alone, so as the phone kept ringing, we made the dance a duet.

Brenda McKay
Finally A Round
Tuitt Red Hatters,
Pell City, Alabama

FUN *on* WHEELS

If you want to be happy, be.

LEO TOLSTOY

I work as the activities director for a health-care center, and some of the women in my care wanted to start a Red Hat Society chapter. I thought the idea sounded like something that could be really great for them, so I started planning. We arranged a meeting and came up with our name—the Red Hat Rollers, since all of the ladies are in wheelchairs or use rolling walkers—and I went shopping for their red hats. Then we met again to decorate them with purple flowers, purple ribbon, and anything else purple we could find. When we were done, the hats looked absolutely tacky. Perfect!

For our first outing, we planned to visit a nearby assisted living facility to attend a poetry reading, which meant that we had to arrange transportation for the eleven of us. The health-care center had a lift van that could accommodate four wheelchairs, with six additional seats. I had just ten Red Hat Society ladies, but all of them were in wheelchairs.

I stared at the van for a while trying to decide how we could possibly fit everyone in the van. In the end, we decided to put four wheelchairs in first, and then take the other ladies out of their wheelchairs to put them in the six seats. We got everyone in—but just barely. That van had never been so packed, before or since. The ladies were laughing so hard at our sardine-like arrangement that they were nearly crying. The van ride was a little disorganized, a little chaotic, and a lot silly, and none of us minded a bit.

Not one of us will ever forget that day, not because the poetry was amazing or the refreshments delectable, but because our group came together for the first time and had a blast doing so. Even though my ladies were all "on wheels," so to speak, and even though they lived in a nursing home and everything seemed to conspire against our having fun, nothing could stop us from being silly and enjoying ourselves.

Christina Bonnett

*The Red Hat Rollers,
Greenwood,
South Carolina*

Recipe for a

Long laughs are bound to occur anytime we get together with our most fun, fabulous friends and family. You never need a reason to throw a party, so why not get everyone together at the first opportunity? Here are four party ideas to get your group giggling.

Classic Movie Night. The options are endless. There's *Bringing Up Baby*, *Some Like It Hot*, all the Pink Panther movies with Peter Sellers, and the original *Father of the Bride*, along with countless other classic, funny movies. Pick two or three favorites and camp out on the couch with some popcorn.

Day Trip. Sometimes the best vacations are only for a day. Load everyone up in your cars and drive to a neighboring county for a Saturday of fun. Tour a garden center or historical site; enjoy some local flavor or visit a zoo. You might even tie it all together with a theme, coordinating goodie bags, lunch spots, and attractions.

The Slumber Party. You're never too old for a slumber party. Just gather all the standard sleepover elements—videos, snacks, goofy pajamas, and a caffeinated beverage or two—and combine with your most energetic friends. It might not be a bad idea to wait until your husband goes out of town; he might not be quite so enthused about hours of girl talk.

Game Night. The beauty of a game night is that you can choose any games you want. You could set up a series of messy games, like egg tosses and water relays, or you could simply serve chips and dip and hunker down at the kitchen table for an evening of card games. The choice is yours.

Of course, the best parties need little organization. Combine good friends with good food, and you're on your way to

laughing up a *storm*.

The JAPAMA PARTY

Laughter is the **sensation** *of feeling good all over and showing it principally in one place.*

JOSH BILLINGS

Like every Red Hat chapter, my group, the Red Hat Flickas ("flickas" means "girls" in Swedish), love to have a good time. We love to put together special events just for us and treat ourselves to a royal bash. Recently, we rented a few hotel rooms and sent out handmade invitations, and our first annual "japama" party became a reality. The curious name "japama" arose when our queen asked if we'd like to have a pajama party sometime and a slip of the tongue caused her to say "japama" instead. We all got a good laugh out of this blunder, and the name stuck.

The queen's room was designated as the party center. We decorated it in red and purple with lighted feather boas, hats, and balloons, and we even found a chocolate fountain. As soon as each partygoer walked in, she received a goodie bag containing a purple kazoo, some chocolate candies, and a new purple T-shirt with a red hat on the front and her special nickname on the back.

Once we'd assembled ourselves and picked up our goodie bags, of course it was time to eat. Entering an eating establishment in Red Hat attire always catches lots of eyes. As we walk past the other diners, we hear comments like, "Here come the Red Hat ladies!" Of course we enjoy the smiles and admiration of staff and guests. We are royalty, after all, the way we see it.

After a few hours of being adored at the restaurant, we buzzed back to the hotel for the ultimate dessert of chocolate fondue and a lovely raspberry wine that went perfectly with the chocolate. The chocolate fueled our party appetite, and soon we were feeling ready for the next thing on our agenda. So when our queen called out, "Tattoos, anyone?" (fake, of course), we hopped up from our seats. Our tattoo artist, the queen, lovingly placed a flower tattoo on the exposed skin of our choice.

As we admired each other's tattoos, we decided it would be a good idea to show them off in the pool. So we got into our swimsuits and then into the pool—wearing our red hats, of course. (We instituted a no-splashing policy to keep the hats safe and dry.)

When our fingers and toes were sufficiently wrinkled, we scurried back upstairs to the room. Unbeknownst to the queen, her court had something amusing up their hats. Each of us had brought an article of clothing to dress up our queen for the evening. As we presented each item, one by one, she put it on, and soon she was wearing two sparkling rhinestone tiaras, huge earrings, and bracelets and pins galore. There was a royal house-dress (with sewn-in unmentionables) and a homemade purple bra made from shoulder pads and red rickrack. She had a flower bush corsage and a bouquet of flowers to carry, while the ugliest furry red slippers I'd ever seen graced her feet.

The **chocolate** fueled our party appetite, and soon we were feeling ready for the next thing on our agenda. So when our queen called out, "**Tattoos**, anyone?" (fake, of course), we hopped up from our seats.

We all laughed so hard we were crying, and the queen, ever a good sport, decided to parade down the hall doing a royal wave as her court followed behind. We stopped for photos along the way and gave the other guests and hotel staff a good laugh.

Our laughs were soon punctuated with a few yawns, so we decided to call it a night and retire to our beds. Given the almost nonstop laughter of the evening, we knew the party had been a success. We had learned new things about each other; we found that those we thought were quiet and reserved were really the most outgoing and funny under the right circumstances. And we learned that all of us were able to laugh at ourselves in a trusting group of friends.

The next morning, we enjoyed a royal breakfast in full regalia in the lobby of the hotel and even started scheming for next year's japama party.

Having fun together and making others happy by spreading our joy is what our group is all about. Call us the queens of fun, fabulous parties.

Sylvia Martins
The Red Hat Flickas,
Iowa City,
Iowa

DO I NEED *an* EXCUSE *to* BE GOOD *to* MYSELF?

Joy is a flower that blooms when you do.

AUTHOR UNKNOWN

I shouldn't have been surprised. Having known Mirt for more than sixty years, I should have known that when she retired, she would not just sit back and wait to be entertained. She had worked tirelessly in our county's administration, organizing senior citizen centers and developing the Meals on Wheels program in our area, and I should have expected that retirement would in no way curb her enthusiasm for making others happy.

Still, I found myself in awe of the way she used her hospitality skills to enrich the lives of all of her friends. She lavished us with love, in the process teaching us a thing or two about how to do the same for ourselves.

Her first summer post-retirement, she threw a garden party with a trunk show theme. She spent months going to rummage sales to pick out items for the affair, and when we arrived on the big day, we saw dressers and trunks standing elegantly in her yard, all dripping with gloves, boots, shoes, boas, hats, purses, jewelry, and sparkly things of all sorts. We lunched at a dozen or so tables set up beside her pool and admired the beautiful things in front of us.

The next year, she used Raggedy Ann and Andy as the theme for our garden fete. She displayed part of her three-hundred-plus collection of the dolls—ranging from a few inches to several feet. They were seated around children's tables, they hung from ladders against trees, and they gazed demurely at us from a cupboard set up in the yard. Again we had lunch, and we laughingly competed to see who could do the best job of coloring a page from a Raggedy Ann and Andy coloring book.

Then came the summer "for the birds." In a bird-themed party, we all received handmade birdhouses and chirped our way through a beautifully decorated back-yard. We sang songs like "When the Red, Red Robin Comes Bob, Bob, Bobbin' Along," among others.

> We took turns opening our gifts, jokingly feigning surprise before explaining why we'd chosen what we did. As I heard the other ladies' stories, such a liberating feeling came over me.

But the summer of "Christmas in July" was the kicker. Mirt announced in the spring that each of us should buy ourselves something we had been wanting for a long time but just didn't feel we should spend the money on. It was like she was giving us permission to give ourselves a special treat.

What a celebration. We walked onto the scene on a rather warm July day and found Mirt serving cider. (We got to keep the mug we chose as a party favor.) There were Christmas trees around her pool, beside the gazebo, and throughout the yard. Every table was lavishly decorated in red and green.

We had been asked to wrap the present and label it with our own name, and each gift was placed under one of the trees when we registered at the welcome table. After a wonderful soup-and-salad luncheon followed by an assortment of Christmas goodies representative of the Scandinavian heritage of our area, it was time to open our gifts—knowing all the while what was inside. There were also several anonymous gifts for our gracious hostess.

We took turns opening our gifts, jokingly feigning surprise before explaining why we'd chosen what we did. As I heard the other ladies' stories, such a liberating feeling came over me. One woman gave herself a pricey pair of tennis shoes she'd been wanting. Another spent a week's worth of groceries for a piece of framed art she'd had her eye on for more than ten years.

One ordered specialty blank checks. And one rented a cabin in the mountains several hundred miles away for her family's next Christmas get-together. All her married life, she'd wanted to spend at least one holiday in the mountains with her family, and this party gave her just the push she needed to book the trip.

After a few years of graciously hosting us, treating us to all kinds of luxuries and treasures, Mirt had given us an even better gift: an excuse to be good to ourselves. We finally felt free to take that trip or buy ourselves that little something special. After all, how disappointed she would have been if none of us had followed through on her party instructions. We were doing it for Mirt—right?

Jackie Tarpinian
Jewels of the Prairie,
Jamestown,
North Dakota

The FUNERAL

*No party is any fun
unless seasoned with folly.*

DESIDERIUS ERASMUS

Our queen mum had always been what they call "well endowed." Not too long ago, she decided to have a breast reduction, resulting in a loss of quite a few pounds. The good Red Hat queen that she is, always looking for a reason to get everyone together for food and fun, she decided to hold a funeral for her very large bras, since they were permanently retiring.

Enlisting the help of her queen of vice, she set about making funeral arrangements. They sent invitations to everyone in our chapter requesting that we come to the queen's house on a certain afternoon to help her with her great loss. In need of a coffin, the queen emptied her large wooden jewelry box and lined it with purple satin. Then she gingerly laid one of the bras inside the box. (She stuffed it first to emphasize the point of the celebration.)

The two made a black wreath to hang on the front door, and a few funeral bouquets stood at attention throughout the queen's living room. (We are nothing if not thorough when we throw a party.) A ribbon reading "Rest in Peace" was draped across the lid of the coffin as it sat on the coffee table. All was ready.

The mourners arrived dressed in Red Hat regalia and were treated to many laughs when the coffin was opened to reveal the stuffed bra. The queen of vice gave the eulogy, which went something like this:

> *"We of the Red Hatters have come today to help our queen mum overcome her recent loss. A great loss it was. She lost not one, but two bosom buddies. She is comforted by her memories. Didn't they always stand up for her when others let her down? And were they not always out front pointing the way? They were the best floaters at her water aerobics class, and when she tap danced, they danced up a storm with her. They definitely had their titillating moments at parties, and they very nearly made it into Ripley's Believe It or Not.*

So today we say good-bye knowing that what was, is no more, and our queen must move on to a smaller view of the future. We wish her good luck."

When she finished, there wasn't a dry eye in the house—though perhaps for different reasons than at most funerals. After taking pictures for posterity, we adjourned to lunch. For dessert, we each had two iced cupcakes set side by side on a plate, a tribute to our queen's fallen bosom buddies.

Merle Northam
The Vintage Bells,
Ilderton, Ontario
Canada

BUNCHES *of* FUN

Creative **experiences** *can be produced*
regularly, consistently, almost daily
in people's lives. It requires enormous
personal **security** *and openness*
and a **spirit** *of adventure.*

STEPHEN R. COVEY

I guess you could say I'm into themes. During my thirty-two years of teaching third grade, I went with a "grape" theme like crazy: I spray-painted all the furniture purple, and I filled my classroom with grape-shaped everything, accumulated through years of gifts from students and determined thrift store shopping on my part. When I married Mr. Welch, he conveniently lent his name to my grape theme.

Each year on the first day of school, I played "I Heard It Through the Grapevine," and my class wore T-shirts that I ordered for each student, featuring grapes (of course) and proclaiming: "Mrs. Welch's Class—Best of the Bunch!" For the first month of school, I wore my so-called uniform of grape-themed clothes, shoes, and jewelry, and I always, always graded papers with purple ink. I guess it's no surprise that I became known as "the grape lady." When I go for a theme, I do it up big.

What I liked about my grape theme is that it gave the kids something to bond around and it taught them to be themselves at their flamboyant best. Besides, it was fun. So when I faced retirement, I wondered where I'd find another creative outlet.

Fortunately, I found just the right place to pour out my creative energy: the Red Hat Society chapter I joined a short while before retiring. The fabulous ladies I met in Caught Red Hatted encouraged me to be my theme-crazy self. Together we embraced that sense of fantasy and fun I tried to teach my students. Red Hatters play in an adult world that doesn't allow the freedom to play or express oneself without fear, and I knew from the start that I would fit right in with that philosophy.

As the time drew near for my retirement party, I wanted to throw a wild, joyous party as a tribute to my newfound sisters. This would be no stuffy occasion like so many other retirement parties. I was determined to spice things up.

And so, as the time drew near for my retirement party, I wanted to throw a wild, joyous party as a tribute to my new-found sisters. This would be no stuffy occasion like so many other retirement parties. I was determined to spice things up "grape lady" style.

I had always said I would die at my desk grading papers. So I borrowed the school's resident plastic skeleton, dashing it out to my car in a big black garbage bag so as not to spoil the surprise. At home I dressed it up as me: purple clothes, purple whistle, school badge—and a sassy red hat. I took "her" to my classroom, put her in my purple desk chair, and wheeled her into retirement. At my party, I introduced her as the death of my former self, the red hat symbolizing the birth of the newly retired (and loving it) me.

The party was a hit; not a single soul was bored. As gifts, I received a purple glass apple (the office staff had searched high and low to find it), as well as a beautiful friendship quilt. Each staff member had decorated a square for me with lots of red hats and purple grapes galore. It was a fitting closure to a lifetime career, celebrating the end of the old and the beginning of a reinvented me.

These days, when my Red Hat chapter needs a theme luncheon or when we dress up as a group for conventions, I am on the scene in full force. My identity shifts from the Grape Lady to Madame Butterfly (complete with butterfly wings) to Karen Miranda, who wears a fruity headdress.

I feel free to be myself—whichever self suits me that day. This freedom came to me thanks to my Red Hat sisters, who love the surprises of my many incarnations. Thanks to them, retirement has not been a slide to the grave but an exciting adventure uniting older women together. We wear our red hats proudly, unleash our creativity, laugh loudly, nurture each other and ourselves, and refuse to be invisible.

Fifty-something and retired is a wonderful place to be. It opens the possibility to be the "you" that you've always hoped to become. As my friend Madame Butterfly often urges her Red Hat sisters: "Kick open that chrysalis, gal, and fly!"

Karen Welch
Caught Red Hatted,
Glendale, Arizona

The SHOW MUST GO ON

It is not true that people stop pursuing dreams because they grow old, they grow old because they stop pursuing dreams.

GABRIEL GARCIA MARQUEZ

As I reached my golden years, I found that I couldn't wait for retirement. Bring on the empty nest syndrome, I thought. My co-workers often asked if I had plans for retirement. I would just smile and say, "Why, I plan to enjoy life more and have more fun."

When I finally did retire, I decided to seek out a Red Hat Society chapter. I wanted to make the best of my life, and from all I had read, I thought the Red Hatters might be just the right connection.

I had my first Red Hat experience when I attended a Christmas in July party, where I took a pledge and met fifty-five new Red Hat friends. From the first moment I walked in, I stood in awe of the creativity of everyone's hats and spectacular purple outfits. I knew I had found just the right group for loving life with style and flair. We were going to have fun, that was for sure.

> I felt free to entertain and laugh and sing and make a crowd roar with laughter and applause. What can I say? I'm a born performer.

We didn't waste any time. After our delicious lunch, the ladies at my table and I started scheming to get some sort of performance act together. Since no one seemed too shy, I suggested we dress as the California Raisins and sing "I Heard It Through the Grapevine."

And so, at our very next gathering, six of us arrived dressed in purple tunics with faux grapes on our heads, white gloves and sneakers, and oversize sunglasses, with ropes of green vines connecting us. We marched in, and the crowd loved us. The next time we did our number, we turned into the Grapes of Wrath at our Halloween social and danced to "The Monster Mash." The group laughed long and loud at our antics.

As they laughed, I felt as though I had finally found a niche in life. Growing up in a family of seven, I had so many family responsibilities, and there was never enough time or opportunity to do the things I wanted. In addition, young ladies in my day

I'm a *born* performer

were not even allowed to ride bicycles or do many things the boys could do. I played the violin with a symphony orchestra because it seemed like the proper thing to do, but it never did quench my thirst to perform.

Now, as a retiree and empty nest dweller, I felt free to entertain and laugh and sing and make a crowd roar with laughter and applause. What can I say? I'm a born performer.

Our adventures in show business continued. At our summer picnic, about fifty of our Red Hat Chicks gathered in a private picnic area to eat and ride on the swings and play water games. Again our group performed. This time we dressed as chicks, complete with soft yellow outfits and strap-on beaks. We waddled out behind a large umbrella, and soon our audience saw that we had armed ourselves with water bottles with which to squirt the onlookers while we sang "Singing in the Rain." We even tossed a few water balloons, resulting in much squealing and laughing. Everyone got a little wet, but no one minded the splash of cool water on that scorching summer day.

The highlight of my year, though, was my debut as an Elvis impersonator. For a Red Hat party, I convinced two friends to be my doo-wop girls, and I dressed as Elvis. We burst onstage singing "Hey, Big Spender" and "Blue Suede Shoes." Yes, I dyed my shoes blue, and I donned a sparkling white jumpsuit with the collar turned up, colorful scarves, a pompadour wig, sunglasses, and a cape of white satin with gold sequins. When I looked into my audience, I saw eyes wide with surprise and mouths open in laughter.

After that performance, I was dubbed the Wackiest Woman of our already wacky chapter, and I considered the title a compliment. This fall I have been appointed queen of our hidden talent show, and my sisters and I are plenty busy discussing who we'll be and what we'll wear. Some of our new acts include the Spike Jones Band, the Andrews Sisters, Carmen Miranda, and the Ziegfeld Follies. About twenty-five ladies will take part in this extravaganza, some of whom have real talent, although talent is by no means a requirement. We'll make our costumes, arrange the music, and do our best to knock them dead.

I think I've discovered the fountain of youth: my friends and I are too busy socializing, singing, dancing, going on

> The highlight of my year was my debut as an **Elvis** impersonator. I convinced two friends to be my doo-wop girls, and I dressed as Elvis.

exciting trips, or playing games to moan and groan about our ailments and aches and pains, and that keeps us young. The opportunities to laugh and play with my sisters have reawakened my inner child; I feel as though I can pursue all my potential and be anything I want to be in this stage of my life.

In the words of E. E. Cummings, growing up into who you really are takes courage. My sisters have given me that courage and an outlet to be my sparkling self, and that is a dear, dear gift.

Alice Woodford
Satellite Red Hat Chicks,
Philadelphia,
Pennsylvania

FRIENDSHIP GETS BETTER AFTER FIFTY

There's nothing quite as good as talking to a friend you've known for years—except maybe talking to a friend you feel as if you've known for years. A friendship between sassy, classy women means support for those hard times, companionship as we enter new chapters of life, and of course plenty of raucous laughter.

Chapters of life

A LOST SOUL

No winter lasts forever;
no spring skips its turn.

HAL BORLAND

Divorced at my age? This was not fair. As I reviewed the past thirty-four years, I realized that I had done nothing for myself in years—I'd poured my energy into loving, nurturing, supporting, and encouraging my family. Now I felt like I'd lost everything. I had few friends of my own and this horrible feeling of having no purpose.

How was I going to navigate this new life status? Where on earth was I going to find friends to confide in, laugh with, and lean on? I felt completely alone in this strange, new world, and I wasn't sure how I could pick myself up and get out of this rut.

I experimented with group after group for singles and those newly single and found them either unhelpful or unwelcoming to newcomers. I sank under the realization that I should have been building relationships alongside my family responsibilities all these years. By nurturing my family and neglecting my own physical and emotional health, I had failed myself. Was it too late to mend the past?

Eight months later, a new wind blew into my town. An acquaintance phoned and told me about an informational meeting held by the Red Hat Society. Neither of us knew what this group for women was about or how it operated. But we had a hunch it might be worth our while to check into it.

I walked into a very full meeting room, awed by the sheer number of women who were looking for something new in their lives. By the end of the meeting, I still wasn't quite sure exactly what this organization did, but I was definitely interested in the opportunity to get together with other women about once a month. Perhaps there was hope for my dull life after all.

Starting a Red Hat chapter made my head spin a little, and trying to remember everyone's name stretched my memory more than I thought possible, but what a marvelous time we all shared along the way—laughing, comparing shopping trips for our red hats and purple dresses, and plenty of girl talk, of course. I soon found that I couldn't wait until we met again.

Whenever we entered a shop or café or restaurant in our regalia, heads turned, which made me feel special and distinctive. And with each get-together, I felt the unity between us growing. Each meeting was grander than the last as our laughter and comfort with each other grew. Soon, I noticed that we had begun to bond as sisters. We laughed and cried together. We placed importance on spending time together. I had found that place to belong for which I'd been searching.

> How was I going to navigate this new life status? I felt completely alone in this strange, new world, and I wasn't sure how I could pick myself up and get out of this rut.

Today I preside over the Blushing Red Hat Mamas as queen—or, as I prefer to call myself, Diva of All Divas. My new friends have added to my life in untold ways. There is nothing we would not do for one another. We feel the pain our sisters feel and support one another during trying times.

Currently I am faced with a diagnosis of breast cancer. On the sidelines, cheering me on, are my sister Red Hatters, waving signs of encouragement as they wait eagerly to assist me in any way they can. With love and thoughtfulness, they flood my life with cards, flowers, phone calls, e-mails, prayers, and meals. They are my rock of sanity—as well as the humorous insanity I sometimes need.

I never fear that I will be alone. My sisters are standing beside me always.

I will always be grateful for the soul sisters who came along when I was feeling lost and disconnected. They helped me navigate this new phase of my life, and the place they helped me reach is full of laughter and fun. Their friendship makes me stronger. With them by my side, I know I can handle anything.

Rose Ann Johansen
The Blushing
Red Hat Mamas,
Des Moines, Iowa

Pink Lady Cake

It's bad to suppress laughter.
It goes back down
and spreads to your hips.

DANIEL WORONA

This moist, pretty cake is perfect for sharing with a good friend.

4 eggs

1 cup vegetable oil

½ cup water

1 package (10-ounce) frozen strawberries, thawed and divided

1 package (18-ounce) white cake mix

1 package (3-ounce) strawberry gelatin

3 tablespoons all-purpose flour

1 package (1-pound) confectioners' sugar

Preheat the oven to 275°. Grease and flour a 13 x 9-inch pan. In a large bowl beat the eggs, oil, water, and half the strawberries. In a separate bowl blend together the cake mix, gelatin, and flour. Add this mix to the batter and beat well. Pour into the prepared pan and bake for 1 hour 15 minutes, or until a tester comes out clean. Cool the cake on a rack.

In a medium bowl mix the confectioners' sugar with the remaining strawberries. Use the mixture to frost the cake.

Tony Horton-Whitehead
Crawford County Cuties, Van Buren, Arkansas

$\mathcal{C}$ELEBRATING LINDA

While grief is fresh, every

attempt to divert only irritates.

You must wait till it be digested,

and then amusement will

dissipate the remains of it.

SAMUEL JOHNSON

$\mathcal{T}$onight we're gathering at Linda's house for a much anticipated potluck picnic. We've all prepared our dishes to share and—as usual—we're ready to party. When I arrive, I head straight for the kitchen, pausing to glance at Linda's red hats hanging gaily in the upstairs hallway.

Our event hostesses, Carolyn and Evelyn, are busy arranging games and prizes in the living room. I quickly set up a card table and begin snapping pictures of the partygoers for our scrapbook.

John and Sarah, Linda's husband and daughter, pitch in to arrange chairs on the deck, where we can admire Linda's favorite geraniums while we dine. We're all bustling around as if we're afraid to be still for even a moment.

To tell the truth, I'm a little wary of stillness tonight. I'm afraid that if I'm still for too long, I'll stop thinking the happy, silly party thoughts that always accompany our get-togethers. Instead, I'll gaze at Linda's beautiful hats and think of all the wordless good-byes I whispered in my heart as I watched her cancer progress. And I'll think of how my prayers grew more frantic as I asked God not to take my friend away, then begged Him not to let her linger too long. I'll remember the day six weeks ago that I joined hands with friends and began to pray: "Lord, it breaks our hearts to be here today . . ." I don't want to picture us filing into the church for Linda's funeral, crying with John and Sarah, singing Linda's favorite hymns, serving food to her friends and family. Those images are too new, still too raw to contemplate. I'd much rather keep busy carrying out one of Linda's final wishes.

> I'm afraid that if I'm still for too long, I'll stop thinking the happy, silly party thoughts that always accompany our get-togethers. Instead, I'll gaze at Linda's beautiful hats and think of all the wordless good-byes I whispered in my heart as I watched her cancer progress.

Linda had kept us girlfriends at the center of her life for almost three years. Once she knew the end was near, she dearly wanted to have us over for one more celebration. She left us too soon for that, but John asked us to have the party anyway. So here we are, celebrating Linda, one of the most fun, beautiful, dignified ladies any of us have ever known. As more people come in, the conversation quickly becomes lively, even a little rowdy.

Suddenly, it's okay to say Linda's name out loud and laugh, all in the same breath. Grieving together is a relatively new experience for all of us. Maybe the laughter will make her absence a little less sharp, a little less painful.

As we start the first game, some stragglers arrive—best friends Beth and Leslie. We flock to Leslie, who has been struggling with her own illness. I cannot even begin to imagine the effort it must have taken for her to be here, and I have to hold back tears when she presents me with a carefully arranged bundle of memorabilia to place in our long-neglected scrapbooks. Beth is wearing her usual serene smile, but in her eyes I see echoes of her own unspoken good-byes. And here comes Clara, bringing her sister Cathy to meet us.

Dinner progresses and the games resume. Clara and I win the dress-up relay. I place a distant third in the bubble-blowing contest, which means I don't have to scrape very much gum off my face. The laughter gets louder, longer, and more genuine, and I'm joining in more freely. My heart lifts as I think, *Linda would have loved this!*

Soon the sky grows dark, and mosquitoes begin to disrupt the party. All around the deck, laughter continues to ring out even as the party disbands. We depart in twos and threes, still laughing. In just weeks our hearts will break again when Leslie leaves us. Still reeling, we'll support Clara through the grief and shock of Cathy's sudden passing. We'll have to learn how to heal all over again, how to find our rhythm in moving through life's good and bad times together. But tonight our hearts are light and our spirits are hopeful as we remember the life and sparkle of one of our dearest sisters.

Clare Dunn
Simply Red
Richmond,
Virginia

A GIFT for JESSE

We acquire the **strength** *we have overcome.*

RALPH WALDO EMERSON

For a long time, I felt as though the world wasn't quite right. Jesse's birthday came and went. Holidays lost their luster and filled me with memories of what they were like before. Memorial Day found me visiting a gravesite, and Mother's Day found me weeping alone in my room. Anyone who has lost a child knows that you never get over it; you simply get through it one day at a time.

As the years passed, I grew restless. I wanted to do something for my wonderful seventeen-year-old son, Jesse. I wanted to do something—I *had* to do something—to honor his memory and share his special spark of life with the world.

Eight years after his death, a door opened for me to do just that. When Jesse died, he gave the gift of life to more than sixty people by donating organs and tissues. As soon as I heard about the Five Points of Life cycling tour—a three-thousand-mile trek from Ottawa, Canada, to Miami, Florida, to promote awareness of the need for tissue donation—I knew I wanted to take part.

Out of four hundred applicants, eleven other riders and I were chosen. Each of us had a personal connection with one of the "five points": whole blood, apheresis (a specific blood component), bone marrow, cord blood (blood collected from a baby's umbilical cord), and organs and tissue. My connection to organ donation, of course, was my Jesse. He is my hero, and the hero of those who received his gifts.

Before the event, I posted the news of the cycling tour on an online discussion board. I just wanted to share a little about the event and why I was participating; I didn't expect these dear people from all over the country to bring tears of joy and sorrow to my eyes.

"Avon Lady" spoke of her husband, Forrest, who received a lifesaving kidney six years earlier. He had suffered on dialysis for more than four years, but has persevered with no signs of rejection since his transplant.

"Kaysperks" related that her husband donated his corneas, which were received by two very grateful ladies who were able to see their grandchildren for the first time. What a meaningful gift for her husband to leave behind.

"Lady Luvalot" shared that her twenty-eight-year-old daughter was patiently waiting for a badly needed liver transplant. Likewise, "Irish Queen" was praying for her twelve-year-old

granddaughter, Sarah,
who needed a new heart.

"Lady Karen" shared the joyous news of her son, Chris, who received a lifesaving liver when he was seven. Now he was twenty-five and "dancing circles" around everyone else, enjoying life to the fullest, she said. Every day, she told us, she thanked God and the parents who made such a heart-wrenching decision at such a tragic time.

"Queen Bee Sharona" had a story with a different slant. At the age of fifteen her son, now thirty-six, received a kidney from his father, a living donor. Sharona was waiting to hear if she might be a donor for her son as well.

But the most touching response came from "Chestergal," a woman named Sheila who quickly became my friend. Her precious daughter, Brenda, had passed away only a week before my posting appeared on the Web site. Sheila generously donated Brenda's corneas and tissue. Knowing the pain Sheila was experiencing, I felt the need to contact her privately and in some way try to help her through her grief journey. We exchanged many e-mails and phone calls in the weeks that followed and forged a bond that kept us both going.

Across the miles, these women gave me the resolve to finish the race in honor of my son. They gave me the knowledge that his life had made a difference and that what I was doing for him would make a difference too.

So what can I do for you, Jesse, my sweet boy? My friends and I will remember you and all the others who had the courage to say yes when they were called upon to give of themselves. All of you live on in more than just our memories. You live on in others.

Jesse, for all the gifts that you gave others, this is my gift to you.

Connie Koch

Mad Red Hatters,
Whiteman Air Force
Base, Missouri

HEALING FRIENDS

A good friend

is cheaper than therapy.

AUTHOR UNKNOWN

"You have got to join the Red Hat Society!" a much younger acquaintance of mine gushed one morning with so much enthusiasm I wondered if she'd had espresso injected directly into her veins. My own caffeine jolt, on the other hand, hadn't quite kicked in. I cut my eyes over at her, just daring her to say the next part. "My mom is, like, your age, and I just know you'd really love it."

I contemplated throwing a wedge of biscotti at her, but I hadn't had breakfast yet. Sometimes the need for nourishment—even if it's all carbs—takes precedence over the need to squash someone's enthusiasm. "Just how old do you think I am?" I asked with astonishing sweetness, considering how much I wanted to pummel her. We Southern belles are taught early on about killing with kindness.

"Well, my mom is, I don't know, about sixty. She's really old."

That's it, I thought. Time to make appointments with a color-ist, a dermatologist, a waxer, a personal shopper. I might even consider a face-lift. "Darlin', I'm not even fifty!" I informed her. I'm sure that if she looked closely at my hands, she might have seen sharp claws begging to be freed.

She made a noise of surprise, and the claws grew ever sharper. "They have a program for ladies who are almost fifty—they're called Pink Hatters. They wear pink and lavender while the *older* ladies wear red and purple."

I silently cursed her to have trench-deep wrinkles and gray hair at thirty. "I don't know. I just don't think that's for me." But I had seen the gatherings of Red Hatters and deep down inside I envied all the fun they appeared to be having. Of course, there was no way I'd tell *her* that.

I was new to the area and newly married. Lots of factors—including and especially a terrible relationship that had taken up the last twenty-eight years of my life—had left me with zero confidence in all areas, from making friends to looking in the mirror. Just the thought of going out with a large group to a public place made me so anxious, with hot flashes so intense, I wanted to strip off all my clothes and jump into the nearest fountain.

And so, even though the idea of grand days out with fun-loving ladies sounded blissful, I didn't know if I could find the courage.

But a few nights later, I gathered my resolve and forced myself to sit down at my computer, search out the Red Hat Society Web site, and contact a local chapter that was accepting new members. I soon heard back from their queen mother. They were planning a tea party outing and offered me an invitation.

How do I get myself into these things? I groaned inwardly.

With anxiety screaming in my ears, I decorated a pink hat with matching feathers and hydrangeas and bought a boa and a lavender blouse. I nervously drove to the meeting place and waited. No red hats to be seen. I waited a little longer. Still no hats. I was receiving curious stares at my hat and boa and had begun to contemplate hiding behind a tree—and then I saw them. Vibrant red hats, brilliant purple clothes: this had to be my group. I took a deep breath and went to introduce myself, feeling a little like I might throw up.

The queen mum suggested we all go in her SUV since we were driving a long distance, while I wondered where I'd put my anxiety medicine. I bravely forced a smile and climbed in.

It took me a while to realize that these women weren't going to torture me; they were a lot like me, actually. Some had grandkids and had been through divorces, some had gotten remarried, some had cancer and anxiety attacks. Slowly I began to realize I wasn't the only woman alive to carry a few battle scars. I didn't feel so out of place and I even began to have fun.

The elegant hat and fancy feathers also gave me a feeling of playing a role onstage, so if the real me didn't want to come out and play, the actress could. And soon the real me did want to come out and play, and she made all kinds of new friends. The anxiety became less and less and the old, happy me came out—the me that loved my face and body and hair and being a grand-ma. My wounds were healing; these fabulous women were making a difference.

My husband and I have since moved to another town, and I started a new chapter of the Red Hats. I am the queen, Queen Nella Fantasia. I still have anxiety attacks—I've even threatened to jump into a fountain or two—but I think my name says it all: Fantasia, *fantastic*. My first Red Hat sisters made me feel fantastic, and now I want to share the love. Our group is focused on reaching out to women who are hurting from bad relationships, recovering from a physical illness, or just feeling lonely. We're out to prove that friendship and a little "hattitude" can make a big difference.

LaNell Koenig-Wilson
Rocky Mountain Red
Red Hat Tamales,
Longmont, Colorado

A Whole New Me

The key to change is to let go of fear.

ROSANNE CASH

I was always a bit of a wallflower, leery of unfamiliar social situations and hesitant to speak up in groups. But when I decided to start a chapter of the Red Hat Society in honor of my best friend's seventieth birthday, the new friends I met somehow brought out a whole new side of me. Since our inception, I have found myself doing things I never would have predicted.

I have worn a purple wig with fried eggs on my head (don't ask) and laughed while complete strangers took my picture.

I have led my group—all wearing flashy red ball caps with red boas sewn to them—in a raucous cheer in front of a whole lot of other silly ladies.

I convinced the general manager of a local theater that the show *Big Purple Undies* would be good for business and, with the help of my dames, sold out the theater.

I somehow convinced friends to pose nude (with only our backs exposed to the camera) for a poster that appeared on a marquee in our downtown theater.

And I have found myself standing onstage at a theater addressing the audience and have been interviewed on TV with some semblance of composure.

My lovely ladies have given me a confidence and assurance I never knew I had. When you have friends with whom to share your life, the good times and the bad with plenty of silly moments thrown in, don't be surprised if a whole new woman is born, one with confidence, boldness, and lots of joy.

Carol Betush

The Rebellious
Elegant Dames,
Redding, California

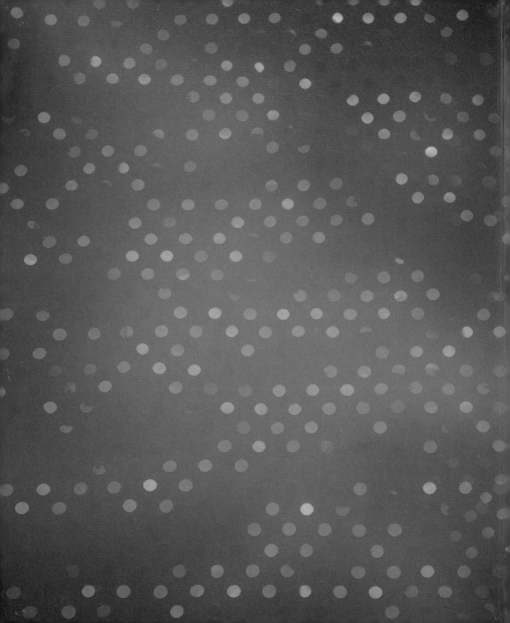